THE RANCH HOUSE

WITHDRAWN

Clockwise from top left: Rickey's Studio Inn, 1953, Palo Alto, California. Ernest J. Kump & Associates, architect. Ranch style proved as effective in commercial and public buildings as in homes. • Cattle skulls, lariats, wagon wheels, spurs, and other motifs of the American West provided an evocative, ornamental system for the Ranch House. • El Rancho Shopping Center, Santa Cruz, California. The Ranch style was also adapted for larger complexes of buildings. • Each wood stud in the prefabricated kit of parts developed by Cliff May and Chris Choate for their tract homes was imprinted with a patent notice. • Antiquated wagon wheels found new roles as both ornamental and functional elements in Ranch houses. • Garbage disposal magazine advertisement from 1955 • At Rickey's Studio Inn, the leisurely sprawl of this motel's wings in landscaped grounds echoes the comfortable way that working ranches blended with nature. • In this glass magazine advertisement from 1948, the tableau of a soldier's ambiguous return from World War II to a new house and a new modern lifestyle is eerily unsettling. • El Rancho Shopping Center, Santa Cruz, California. As a key component of suburban architecture in the 1950s, the Ranch style easily embraced the automobile. • Douglas Fir Plywood Association brochure from 1957 featuring the range of Ranch Houses, from post-and-beam Contemporary Style to Traditional.

El Rancho
Shopping Center

PROTECTED BY
PENDING PATENTS
CLIFF MAY AND
CHRIS CHOATE

THE RANCH

HOUSE

BY ALAN HESS   PHOTOGRAPHY BY NOAH SHELDON   HARRY N. ABRAMS, INC., PUBLISHERS

Editorial Concept Development and
    Project Management: Richard Olsen
Copy Editing and Editorial Assistance: Sigi Nacson
Designer: Russell Hassell
Production Manager: Justine Keefe

Front Cover: Sensing House, 1955, Phoenix, Arizona. Allied Builders.
Endpages: Advertising billboard for Hillsdale development, 1940.
Highway 101 and 31st Avenue, San Mateo, California. David Bohannon,
developer.
Pages 4-5: Toluca Wood, 1941. San Fernando Valley, California.
Marlow-Burns, developer. Cliff May, designer.
Back Cover: Donaldson House, 1957, Phoenix, Arizona. Ralph Haver,
Architect. Fred Woodworth, builder.

Published in 2004 by Harry N. Abrams, Incorporated, New York

Library of Congress Cataloging-in-Publication Data

Hess, Alan.
The ranch house / by Alan Hess ; photography by Noah Sheldon.
    p.   cm.
Includes bibliographical references and index.
ISBN 0-8109-4346-8 (hardcover)
1. Ranch houses. 2. Architecture–United States–20th century.
I. Sheldon, Noah. II. Title.

NA7208.H47 2004
728'.373'0973–dc22

2004003147

Image Credits: Courtesy of Bohannon Development Company,
pp. 2-3, 39, 40 (left, right), 41, 42 (top, bottom), 43, 46, 47 (right);
Courtesy of Alan Hess, pp. 23, 24 (top), 49 (left, right), 58 (bottom),
66 (left, right), 67 (left, right), 68 (all), 70, 71, 72, 73, 74, 75, 76, 79;
Courtesy of Curtis Horton, p. 19; Courtesy of John F. Long Properties
LLP, pp. 55, 56, 57, 58 (top), 59, 60, 77; Courtesy of Randell Makinson
(Drawing by Donald Woodruff), p. 21 (left, right); Courtesy of Richard
Olsen, pp. 20, 32, 34, 128 (left, right), 129, 130 (left, right), 131 (left,
right); Courtesy of William Krisel, pp. 61, 62, 63, 64-65; Copyright
© 2005 Paul Rocheleau, p. 48; Copyright © 2005 Julius Shulman,
pp. 45 (left, right), 52, 53; Copyright © 2005 Roger Sturtevant
Collection, The City of Oakland, The Oakland Museum, pp. 26, 44,
47 (left); Copyright © 2005 Alan Weintraub/Arcaid, p. 24 (bottom);
Courtesy of Royal Barry Wills Associates, Inc., Architects, p. 36;
Copyright © 2005 David R. Williams Collection, The Alexander
Architectural Archive, The General Libraries, The University of Texas
at Austin, pp. 28, 31.

Printed and bound in China
10 9 8 7 6 5 4 3 2 1

Harry N. Abrams, Inc.
100 Fifth Avenue
New York, N.Y. 10011
www.abramsbooks.com

Abrams is a subsidiary of
LA MARTINIÈRE
GROUPE

CONTENTS

ACKNOWLEDGMENTS

Great appreciation goes out to the many people who supported and aided the research and production of this book. First, the Ranch House owners who shared their homes and their experiences; their appreciation and care for their homes over the years confirms the continuing livability and validity of this architecture. They include Connie Adams, Enis Antrim, Mary Barrett, Peggy and Wayne Bemis, Patrice and Keith Blackpool, John and Ann Burdine, Robert and Nina Burgeno, Ann and Fred Christiansen, Paul Des Jardins, Maxine Donaldson, Hugh Evans, Sam Ford, Cy Gomberg, Susan Gould, Bonnie Gross, Nancy Hanley, Bob Lewis, Steve Lamb, Janna Parker Lee, Chris and Monica Miller, Marc and Lisa Mills, Fran and Peter Morris, Jay Pigford, Sandra Rhodes, Celia and Barbara Risk, Jim Rogers, Cheryl Sensing, Richard Sherman, Scott Spier, Amanda Thompson, Robert Wagner, Jennifer Warren and Roger Gimbel, and Mr. and Mrs. Charles Williams.

For a subject neglected as long as this one, it proved invaluable to be able to talk with some of the architects and developers (or their families) involved directly in the design and development of Ranch Houses. For generously sharing their time, thoughts, and archives, I thank Peter Choate, William Krisel, John F. Long, Frances Bohannon Nelson, and Dan Saxon Palmer. For other essential assistance, my thanks to Elizabeth Applegate, Ron Beeler, Bruce Burman, and Peggy Minor of the Rolling Hills Community Association.

Also indispensable to this project were the professional and ingenious archivists and librarians who helped to fill in many of the gaps where the original architects or developers were not available. Thanks to Neil Bethke and the Charles Van der Ahe Library at Loyola Marymount University, Marjean Blynn and the Palos Verdes Library, Beth Dodd and the Alexander Architectural Archive at the University of Texas at Austin, Bruce Emerton and the University

Library at California Polytechnic University at Pomona, Kurt Helfrich and the University Art Museum at the University of California, Santa Barbara, Scott Jorgenson of the Jorgenson Collection, Bill McHarris and the Oakland Museum, Diane Sheardown and Linda Martorana of The David D. Bohannon Organization, Dace Taube and the Doheny Library at the University of Southern California, and the Bancroft Library's Henry J. Kaiser Collection at the University of California.

Many colleagues and friends helped in discussing ideas and supporting my research as I pieced together the broad scope of this story. My gratitude to Debbie Abele, John Balzar, Jim Benjamin, Ken Bernstein of the Los Angeles Conservancy, David Bricker, Robert Bruegmann, Linda Colliatie, John English, Stephen Fox, Dale and Shirley Furman, Grady Gammage, Jr., Daniel Gregory, George and Mary Hartmeyer, Jim Heimann, Greg Hise, Herb and Deborah Huebsch, Dwayne Jones, Jean Mendle, Chris Nichols, Merry Ovnick, Daniel Paul, Richard Peters, Julius Shulman, George Thomas, Marc Treib, Donald Waldie, Elizabeth Wilson, and Sally Woodbridge.

Special gratitude goes to Richard Olsen, my editor at Harry Abrams, Inc., for inviting me to tackle a subject which broadened my perspective on twentieth-century architecture; to Barbara and Charles Hess for raising me in Ranch Houses; and to noted authority John Beach for first impelling me to look at Ranch Houses.

—Alan Hess

The editor extends special thanks to Kris Olsen whose knowledge of the architecture of the Phoenix area and appreciation of the Ranch House enabled the inclusion of several of the houses featured in this book.

Opposite: Burgeno House, 1953, Long Beach, California, Cliff May, designer; Chris Choate, architect. The car was a key element in Ranch House design. It allowed residents to live in sylvan suburbs, away from crowded cities and smoky factories. In turn, the Ranch House accommodated itself to the car, notably in integrating garages into its design.

The Ranch House

The Ranch House is a twentieth-century invention. From sprawling ramblers under cedar-shake roofs to the minimal ranches of mass-produced housing tracts; from sleek contemporary varieties to middle class ranches on quarter acre lots with board-and-batten siding, diamond window mullions, and dovecotes over the garage; from Colonial, Spanish, and French Country ranches to the open-plan ranch of family rooms and sliding glass doors—the ranch is the primary housing type from a period of American national expansion. It is the face of the suburb, whether beloved or reviled.

On Devonshire Avenue, in the San Fernando Valley, California, Camelback Road in Scottsdale, Arizona, Quarton Road in Bloomfield Hills, Michigan, in Hoffman Estates in suburban Chicago, the Ranch House is a national architecture that populates large swaths of America's cities. Beginning in the 1950s, the Ranch House became one of the most widespread, successful, and purposeful of American housing types—a shelter of choice for both movie stars in the San Fernando Valley and aerospace factory workers in Lakewood. The Ranch House matches the philosophical potency of the bungalow, it outstrips the brownstone in numbers, and it challenges the log cabin in mythic power. As the suburbs expanded, the Ranch House grew out of a search for a homestead in nature. It has since been reshaped by the modern appliances and lifestyles of the post-World War II generation, mass produced by organizational and technological improvements fostered during the war, and tailor made for the emerging trends of consumerism. Its rich image has been promoted and spread overtly by popular magazines and subliminally by movies and television.

Ranches were evocative of place: specifically, of the American West—from Texas to California and from Montana to Arizona—and, later, of a more legendary West that was invoked in the movies and television. Although this latter sense of place was freed from an actual geographic setting, it still conjured a place of prairies and buttes, that proved powerful in selling houses.

At the beginning of the twentieth century it would not have been easy to see the cultural, technological, and economic forces that would coalesce as the Ranch House in the 1950s. It took more than one unlikely leap to transform an industrial, rural architecture of the nineteenth century—which served the hardworking ranchers in harsh climates on the plains, mountains, and valleys of the West—into a suburban mass-produced house in the twentieth. The upheaval of World War II, the transforming impact of the media, and the explosion of population and prosperity ultimately gave shape and prominence to the Ranch House.

Although 1950s Ranch Houses may have borrowed the name, board siding, rustic wood details, sun-splashed adobe walls, and ground-hugging profile of its industrious nineteenth-century predecessors, the Ranch House is a thoroughly modern architecture. It may, in fact, be one of the most successfully modern of all; few other residential building types are spread so widely and provide decent housing for so many, chiefly on the strength of modern building techniques, materials, and systems. Modernists had dreamt of this possibility from the beginning, but never achieved it so widely.

As a mixture of historic precedent and Modern design, the twentieth century Ranch House made many adaptations. The Prairie Style, the Usonian house, and the Modern house were all powerful and influential examples of design. Although they did not achieve the dispersion of the Ranch, they presaged the outlines of the classic 1950s Ranch House which emerged: low rambling structures that opened directly onto outdoor patios, ornamented with rustic elements, board-and-batten walls, shake roofs,

Opposite: Donaldson House, 1957, Phoenix, Arizona. The Ranch House was the dominant residence-type of the American Century. Few building types ever housed as many Americans. With prosperity surging, millions of blue-collar laborers suddenly had access to a home of their own, on their own piece of land. Before, most had known only apartments—often situated in crowded cities. The Ranch moderated the strident lines and images of early twentieth-century European Modernism at the same time that it used the liberating power of modern technology to make these homes affordable, as well as reachable in an automobile. The Ranch turned housing into a mass-market commodity, but one that allowed a range of choices in appearance, amenities, and location. Its imagery linked Americans to one of the nation's primal myths. Twentieth century mass media—magazines, movies, and television—spread the look and the lifestyle. It dominated the urban landscape for thirty years.

porches along one entire side of the building, or cut into the mass of the building, wood work, open trusses, unpainted brick walls in kitchens, and more. The open floor plan was also anticipated: living rooms and dining rooms (or dining rooms and kitchens) blended together in an open plan. Living rooms migrated to the rear of the house and opened through picture windows or sliding doors onto the backyard.

The nineteenth-century working Ranch House was a single house or a compound of buildings, situated on a wide-open prairie. The suburban translation of this spaciousness was a broad front lawn, with the long side of the house facing the street, suggesting a large lot. The house formed a wall to protect the rear lot, where family life could exist in a private realm of lawns, gardens, hanging laundry (before the common acceptance of modern clothes driers), pools, and barbecues—all of which created a private home, a private range for family use. The modern Ranch House offered vistas not of the hard work of cattle wrangling, but of the very contemporary twentieth-century preoccupations of recreation and entertaining. Both the Prairie Style house and the Ranch House were thus domesticated with a touch of both practicality and romance—for the uses of late-twentieth century living. Inside, the spaces also suggested expansiveness. Rooms blended into an open plan, and sliding glass doors linked the indoors to the outdoor patio.

This new residential type, developed in the Southwest, represented a moderate modernism, employing current techniques and spaces without a stark modern image. "Here let me disclaim a reactionary point of view," explained architect Royal Barry Wills in 1941, "for I believe in modern houses which come along in pace with the times, but are kept free of the exclusive thought peculiar to the ultra-conservative or the revolutionary,"[1] The blend proved appealing to many homebuyers in the United States in the 1940s through the 1960s. Mass production bestowed affordability. Families could live an open, casual lifestyle in their family rooms, kitchens, and backyards. It was a realistic modernism—with the fruits of technology making architecture easier and more pleasant—not a monastic aesthetic of abstraction. The Ranch House proved that twentieth-century homes did not necessarily have to look like machines, Le Corbusier's

rhetoric not withstanding. Modern technology and historic images could and did coincide.

As noted, the Ranch was also a creature of twentieth-century media, which spread the delights and philosophy—and myth—of suburban life in magazines, movies, and television. The Ranch House was more about a way of living properly in the mid-twentieth century, than a reproduction of any specific prototype. This lifestyle was fleshed out over decades by writers—from Helen Hunt Jackson to Louis Lamour—and promoted and popularized by magazines like *Sunset* and *House Beautiful*, defined in forms by Western architects like William Wilson Wurster and Cliff May, disseminated by the movies and television, and then constructed for the mass market by the emerging home-building industry after World War II. The romance of rustic board-and-batten siding, the pleasures of long front porches, and the illusion of the garage-as-stable mixed freely, inspired by the myths of Ramona and Roy Rogers. Through the media, popular culture invested this utilitarian architecture with an image, changing a rustic building into the consumer's embodiment of the rugged, individualistic cowboy way of life. The cattle and ranching industry of Hispanic California contributed adobe and outdoor fiestas to the Ranch style, but the media and real estate industries gave it a second life of stud walls and barbecues in the twentieth century.

The definition of Ranch has been malleable. In 1900, it meant a rural vernacular building, of interest (like the California Missions) to Arts and Crafts-architects who appreciated its direct use of natural materials. In the 1930s, an increasing fascination with regional architecture developed among leading architects; rustic architecture—with forms of simplicity, the beauty of plainness, and compositions of accretion—expressed an informal lifestyle. In 1950 the Ranch House could be found across the nation and it symbolized, in the eyes of *Sunset* magazine, the ultimate modern home, reflecting a lifestyle of simplicity, privacy, and informality that was close to nature. By 1980, it was a dull, repetitive suburban housing type lacking imagination or style. In fact it was regionally variable; in Arizona, Ranch Houses were concrete block, while in Michigan, they were Colonial or Modern; in New England they were Cape Cod.

Introduction

The elegantly rustic California bungalow and the spatially explosive Prairie Style houses also played a role in the development of Ranch, alongside earlier vernacular adobe and wood vernacular types. By the 1930s, the Ranch style was an accepted part of any respectable architect's repertoire, alongside Tudor, Colonial, and Mediterranean. Architects John Byers, Lutah Maria Riggs, Sumner Spaulding, Paul R. Williams, Cliff May, and others in Southern California carefully rearranged and edited the historic type. In Northern California, the vernacular wood ranch buildings of the region likewise influenced residential design in the work of William Wurster and Gardner Dailey; in Texas the pioneers' stone homes influenced David Williams, John Staub, O'Neil Ford, and others. Interestingly, some of these names were also the leaders of the Modern movement in their regions, and along with more pure Modernists like Harwell Hamilton Harris and Ralph Haver, their work blended the conscious themes of Modernism with an appreciation and understanding of vernacular buildings.

What these architects developed together was a hospitable Modernism. The building's asymmetry revealed that the pieces of the house were thus arranged for practical reasons, not because some pretentious architect wanted to line up the windows to make it look Colonial. Ranch implied a lack of concern for convention and for following fashionable tastes. There is a modesty reflected in its humble materials, a low profile in the shade of the wide eave and the unpainted brick foundation, and a lack of showy portals or grand formal rooms. In 1946, Cliff May praised the unpretentiousness of the Ranch House—an architectural quality that does not sell as well today.

Cliff May's name is linked to Ranch (". . . by far the most skillful practicioner of the Californian ranch-house style," in Brendan Gill's estimate) partly on the momentum of his highly successful self-promotion with *Sunset* magazine.[2] But the roles of other architects were also important in creating this massive phenomenon: William Wurster, Ed Fickett, Chris Choate, Palmer and Krisel, even A. Quincy Jones. Equally significant are the developers—such as Henry J. Kaiser, Fritz Burns, David Bohannon, John F. Long—and the developments; before or contemporaneous with Levittown were Rolling Hills (an upscale community of Ranch houses begun in 1932), San Lorenzo Village, and Panorama City.

The application of modern technology to mass-produced building often came down in a very real sense to the power saw, prefabrication, and organization, marshaling small armies of workers and small arsenals of materials. The Ranch architects were all experimenters, developing many different ways to solve the problem of efficient, marketable, and profitable mass-produced housing. For to become the phenomenon it would, not only did the Ranch have to be mass produced, but mass marketed—a step the Modern architect Walter Gropius never understood.

To create the classic Ranch House of the 1950s, which spread across the country and proved so popular with home buyers and appealing to home builders, to produce the mass-consumer trend of the Ranch which came to define an era, a lifestyle, and state of mind in America, the aesthetic of the Ranch House had to be commodified. That is, it had to be restructured as a building product that could be replicated and sold in mass. As the nexus of post-World War II prosperity shifted into overdrive, the baby boom and the building and populating of the suburbs created the perfect moment for Ranch to make a radical cultural jump. Developers helped weld the style to the astonishing building systems and processes that emerged from rapid, large-scale defense housing developments—thus creating the ideal consumer housing product for the boom times of the 1950s. Ranch was not to be just another style alongside Colonial, Cape Cod, and Tudor. It was to be the vehicle for the design of suburbia and the housing of choice for its time.

Ironically, this type of rambling suburban one-story home that became so identified with the West and its myths may just as easily have been called a Cape Cod. In the hands of Boston architect Royal Barry Wills, Cape Cod homes (enlarged and elongated for modern family life) became an East Coast rendition of the Ranch as he spread the style in magazine publicity and numerous plan books. Mass production tracts also valued the Cape Cod cottage. Green Acres in Valley Stream, Long Island, described as a "wholly planned" community by Chanin Construction Co. in 1946, were all Cape Cods.[3] The homes of the first Levittown on Long Island in 1947 were also simple salt-box Cape Cods, one-and-a-half-story homes, with no eaves and a steeply pitched roof, embodying positive connotations of tradition, security, and acceptability. Cliff May, Ranch prophet of the West Coast, saw the Ranch House as "something like crushed and stretched Cape Cods."[4] Wills was nearly as effective in promoting the Cape Cod on the East Coast as May was in promoting the Ranch House on the West Coast.

Like May, Wills' designs responded to the forces of modern life using more open plans; *Good Housekeeping* presented Will's George W. Cleary House in Duxbury, Massachusetts, in 1953 as "stylistically, Massachusetts Bay Architecture with a leavening of ranch-house design.[5] The rough-sawn siding and shedlike attached garage with roof dipping close to the ground were typical of the local vernacular, yet the elongated plan and combined living room and dining room were similar to Ranch plans across the country. "We find that despite the popularity of the so-called Ranch House the Cape cottage house still has an immense appeal," wrote Wills in one of his many publications in the 1950s.[6]

The Colonial Ranch House was a fixture of the ranch movement across the country, with examples in Pasadena, California, Bloomfield Hills, Michigan, and Connecticut.[7] This blending of Ranch and Colonial styles was described in plan books as well: the "ranch or rambling type of home have been combined with the modern colonial lines of this one-story home" with large picture windows; "the exterior combines the graciousness and dignity of early Colonial architecture with the rambling spaciousness which is so closely associated with the modern western rambling type home."[8]

But the Ranch House as a commodity, as a generic brand (to borrow another cowboy term), was something new, which is always a plus in the marketplace. The Ranch House represented a whole range of powerful images and myths: new possibilities, rugged individualism, self determination, ease and convenience, informality, wide open spaces. The Ranch was after all a product of the West, born of the explosive mid-century growth of that region. It was not the only booming region, of course, but in its newness and size it was emblematic of the national trends. Its architects and

builders were building for new Westerners: "California is the trend setter, the Midwest had no ideas," said Phoenix developer John F. Long, who on a recommendation from his mortgage company frequently traveled to California to observe the latest trends.[9] There would always be a market for Cape Cod, but for the progressive 1950s, the Ranch label triumphed in capturing this spirit of newness.

Along with the freeway, the shopping mall, and the commercial strip, the Ranch House was a prime building block of suburbia as it became the major thrust of urban growth in the United States after World War II.[10] A dream to many, maligned by others, the Ranch became a mixed metaphor in America culture. For some, Ranch became shorthand to identify suburbia and all that its critics detested about it—little boxes made of ticky tacky, ranchburgers, soulless hovels on isolated culs de sac. And yet the reality was more complex, as *Holy Land*, the eloquent memoir of D. J. Waldie, a lifelong resident of such little boxes, testifies.

Though based tangentially and rhetorically on nineteenth-century ranches, the Ranch House took on a contemporary form in custom home designs in the late 1920s and 1930s. But it achieved true impact in the housing boom of the 1950s, as returning veterans moved to the suburbs and looked for their home and piece of land. What the 1950s brought—and what the spread of the Ranch House depended on—was an unprecedented demand for housing. Between 1950 and 1960, Los Angeles's population grew 45%.[11] The pent-up need for new housing—postponed since 1929 and the Depression—was further inflated by the baby boom and a massive shift of the population from inner cities to the new suburban areas, and from east to west.

But that massive change in scale demanded new means of construction, organization, and planning to feed the tremendous demand for housing. The methods of the small-time developer and home builder of the 1920s and 1930s could not possibly meet demand: tracts measured by the hundreds and even thousands, not by the dozens, were now required. However, soon after the Ranches of Lakewood and Panorama sprouted, a myth of suburban soullessness and Ranch House anomie sprang up. But for all the criticism, many Ranch tracts were planned not just as housing, but as

Introduction

communities. Parks, schools, churches, and shopping and recreation centers were often part of the original planning for a site—especially for the larger projects. The almost instant aversion to suburbia among academics had an unfortunate side effect as some of the most brilliant thinkers of the time played little role in shaping the Ranch phenomenon. Today, fortunately, historians have shined a more accurate light on the suburban myth and have revealed a very different picture.[12] Far from being a meaningless, inchoate sprawl, the placement and design of housing tracts, shopping centers, and freeways has often followed a clear logic.

Take one example: Although today the "anonymity" of the Ranch House is criticized in New Urbanist literature—specifically, they criticize the windowless walls frequently turned to the public street—this feature was once considered a progressive idea; tenement reformers abhorred street life, and Ranch tract books boasted about eliminating the front porch where the "old folks sit in their rockers."[13] A house turned away from the street encouraged blessed privacy; a house that turned its face to a delightful backyard of grass, swings, and picnic tables opened up a new world to the former residents of cramped apartments.

New homebuyers in 1946 did not expect to find tenement blocks, front stoops, apartment houses, or row houses when they moved to the suburbs. The single-family home on its own lot made the move from the crowded cities to the spacious suburbs, an improvement in lifestyle. Whether in Lakewood, California, Park Forest, Illinois, or Sharpstown, Texas, the single-story Ranch House (no matter how small) represented an ideal landscape of prosperity, and arrival, both socially and geographically.

Writing of Harwell Hamilton Harris, one of the contributors to the contemporary Ranch House, *House Beautiful* editor Elizabeth Gordon noted in 1945, "Harris looks upon the free-standing, individually owned house as one of the brightest flowers of American culture. He will go to any extreme to avoid sacrificing it to the European design formula of building row or group housing as a means of meeting rising costs. This has called for skillful planning on his part and has resulted in houses often almost diminutive in

size yet possessing the dignity, privacy, and other amenities of houses many times as large."[14]

The Ranch House addressed issues of building in the twentieth century that high-art Modernism for the most part avoided. Mass production of decent housing had long been a dream of Modern architects, and many developed ingenious prefab and panelized systems to achieve it. Yet most of these architects avoided the difficulties and compromises of mass commercial housing and mass marketing that was required to put it into practical use. An untold part of the Ranch House story is the work of architects such as Dan Palmer, William Krisel, and Edward Fickett, and developers such as David Bohannon and John Long, who saw modern techniques through to fruition.

It raises the question: what determines architectural significance: an impact on high-art theory and ideas, or an impact on the built landscape and the buildings in which most people live their lives?

It is time for the Ranch House to take its place in the history of architecture in the twentieth century. Projects far more limited in their impact (like the Case Study program) have ironclad positions in the history books. But the story of the Ranch, transforming acres in almost every city in the nation, has been underplayed. In this historical discrepancy can be seen a bias against mass culture and mass taste, against the adaptations of "pure" modern ideas in order to make them viable. Ironically, these pragmatic concerns are fundamentally functional—the basis of Modernism since the early-twentieth century.

Ranch was not the product of the establishment channels of the architecture profession. A large number of the architects significant to its development were not trained by the traditional academies; rather, direct exposure to vernacular ranches at an early age inspired their interest. Californian Cliff May was a furniture maker and band leader, untrained in architecture, and never a licensed architect; Texan O'Neil Ford's training came through correspondence courses and touring small towns full of small historic houses, many on working ranches, in his Model T. Was there something about their backgrounds that caused them to see qualities in the plain Ranch House that would become generally

popular? Were they interested in ranches because they had not been trained to ignore them? Another prominent contributor to the style, William Wurster, was trained at the University of California, and yet he also opened his eyes to vernacular alternatives in the simplest "unarchitected" buildings. Such unexpected twists often reshape the history of architecture.

The Ranch House turns many assumptions about Modernism upside down. Was it traditional or Modern? Or both? One Modern tenet stated that buildings should reflect local conditions; "A 'Cape Cod' cottage in the San Fernando Valley or a 'ranch' in Maine are obvious absurdities," wrote critic T. H. Robsjohn-Gibbings.[15] And yet the Ranch House redefined "local conditions" for a culture drawn together by national media. Ranch was a nationwide style, found from Vermont to Florida to Texas to Michigan to Arizona to California. In a media-driven era, images and consumer desires were broadly dispersed. If the movies could make John Wayne as popular in Maine as he was in California, why wouldn't a Home on the Range be just as appealing to people nationwide?

The rustic hand-hewn Ranch House, inspired by the Craftsman tradition and the hand-built vernacular, became the epitome of twentieth-century industrial housing, wrangling sophisticated organizational principles, modern materials, and prefabrication to provide decent tract housing. And yet its *appearance* did not express this industrial process, as orthodox Modernism dictated. Its moderate Modernism clung steadily to the age-old desire for the home as cultural symbol, conveying qualities valued by the culture: individuality, closeness to nature, and informality. The Ranch House also redefined the relationship of technology to architecture by abandoning the reliance on sleek machine imagery. It did not celebrate those tools; it used them to create a picture, a story, and a place. In this it paralleled another influential twentieth-century technology, the movies. One goes to the movies to see the story flickering on the screen, not to admire the projector.

And in a manner typical of the twentieth century, the Ranch House embodied an apparent contradiction: It offered the image of individuality in one's own home, one's own piece

of property, in a style evoking the rugged individualism of the West, but it was accomplished through mass production, mass marketing, and mass imagery. The apparent contradictions would seem odd to a profession that created individual custom homes tailored to individuals. But it was also the way of the twentieth century, a perfectly logical evolution. How else could so many have been provided with so much?

Moreover, the Ranch House reflected a mass taste that cut across social class. Western plutocrats such as oilman Frank Phillips, razor blade merchandiser King Gillette, and media mogul William Randolph Hearst used the Ranch style as the preferred style for their country estates. While their Eastern brethren would spend their steel, shipping, or Manhattan real-estate fortunes on imitating chateaux and palazzi, these plutocrats went pointedly rustic, building over-scaled log cabins as luxurious estates. In the same way, the middle class willingly embrace the informal Ranch for their homesteads.

It is time to put the twentieth century in a new perspective. Two well-known programs for mass-produced housing—the Case Study program and the Eichler Homes—usually represent architecture's contributions to the post-war housing crisis. Both are significant, but neither illuminates the whole story. The architects and developers who made design decisions which shaped the suburbs are a large and largely overlooked part of the equation in understanding how post-war suburban metropolises evolved. Their decisions can be criticized, but they must also be rationally understood. They were often responding to the powerful cultural, economic, and social verities of the era. There is more to say about Cliff May's influence than to remark that it is "profound and banal," as does one recent historian.[16]

The quality of design and construction of tract Ranch homes varies, of course. Some were shoddy and ill-conceived. But many were practical and appealing, addressing issues avoided by the custom designs and relatively large budgets of the Case Study houses, or the narrow market niche of the Eichler Homes (he was essentially a successful boutique developer). Perhaps it is unfair to compare architectural apples and oranges. But the manner in which tracts applied modern construction methods and materials, the way they

Introduction

reshaped the house for modern lifestyles and satisfied hundreds of thousands of inhabitants are remarkable accomplishments of architecture and design.

Though not intentionally, the tract Ranch House of the 1950s tolled the end of the architect's role in designing middle-class homes. Despite competitions, programs, and dozens of discussions on the issues in *Architectural Forum* and *Architectural Record*, few architect-designed houses rose successfully to the challenge of applying a decent design to a $10,000 house, something that millions of families in the 1950s aspired to and could only afford. This was the challenge faced squarely by developers such as David Bohannon, Abraham Levitt, John F. Long, and Sam Hoffmann, and a few architects such as Dan Palmer, Bill Krisel, and Ed Fickett. They did not have the luxury of an exclusively well-heeled customer. They could not sidestep the realities of the marketplace.

By the 1970s, the formula changed. Land prices became more expensive. Connected townhouses and two-story homes on smaller pieces of property—often with zero lot lines—were now favored by developers. Rising energy costs made low rambling one-story homes with large picture windows more expensive to maintain. The Ranch image had been dominant for close to thirty years, and changing fashion demanded something new. The ongoing attacks on suburbia turned the prototypical *ranchburger* into a joke with the cachet of a latter-day tenement house. The Ranch died out as a new home style. Today, as property values rise even further, one-story Ranch homes become candidates for demolition as homeowners seek more space on smaller lots. Yet we are also beginning to see evidence of a renewed interest in the lifestyle, the forms, and the images of the Ranch—thus inciting controversies as its neighborhoods are slated for removal or remodel.

The Ranch House is not a simple thing to define. Nineteenth-century definitions referred to the economic function of the buildings, not to any single style. In the mid-twentieth century, when Ranch was a real-estate commodity, assessors, developers, architects, and critics all used the term to apply to a range of different sizes, structures, and types. The term Ranch changes in the literature of the times according to era and context. A Ranch can be compact or sprawling, brick or wood, on the prairie or in suburbia, reflecting the tradition of the Chicago bungalow or the Spanish hacienda. In 2003, the term was even used to refer to an apartment flat—known as a "lower ranch" on the ground floor and an "upper ranch" on the fourth floor.

Following are a set of characteristics by which the Ranch House was usually identified in its day, and which still hold true. If a building includes a majority of these characteristics, it is a Ranch, but it does not need to include them all:

A Ranch Definition

- A one-story house with a low-pitched, gabled, or hipped roof, with wide eaves
- A house of general asymmetry (in contrast to Colonial symmetry)
- A house with a general horizontal emphasis (in forms, or in materials emphasizing horizontality)
- An open-interior plan blending functional spaces
- A house with a designed connection to the outside (this can include a U-shaped plan that embraces a terrace patio, sliding glass doors, picture windows, a front porch, etc.)
- A house with informal or rustic materials or details (board-and-batten siding, high brick foundations, dovecotes, Dutch doors, shake roof, barn door garage doors, exposed rafter beams, exposed truss ceilings, etc.) Ornamental elements can include Rustic, Spanish, French, Colonial, or other traditional styles. Or, with simpler Modern detailing, it can be a Contemporary Ranch House.
- A house whose plan is rambling and suggestive of wings or additions

Rancho Santa Margarita, c. 1849, San Diego County, California. The basic gabled shape of the Ranch House found expression in adobe, log, stone, and wood frame throughout the American West in the nineteenth century. A porch ran along the front in response to the climate, providing shade that cooled the interior and a cooler place to sit outside on hot days. This particular hacienda played a role in transmitting the image of the house on a working ranch of the nineteenth century directly into the sub-urban Ranch House of the twentieth: designer Cliff May visited this home, owned by a family member, as a child.

Preludes to the Suburban Ranch House

Working Ranches

The walls of Rancho Camulos (1848) in Ventura County, California, are made of thick adobe. When the Spanish arrived in California, they used mud mixed with straw—both plentiful local materials—to make bricks that were then laid up by Native American labor. Finishing layers of mud and white-wash created a smooth surface to help rainwater run off. The sturdy walls supported beams that held roofs of red tile.[1]

The first small cabin of the Harrell Ranch House (1875) on the V Bar Ranch in Scurry County, Texas, was built of local stone, but a larger addition was built using a simple and widely used construction method: wide planks nailed side by side to a wood frame, with smaller boards nailed over the gaps between the large planks.

The tin-roofed porch of Hacienda del Cayetano (1919) in Tubac, Arizona, is an outdoor room and corridor lined with half a dozen French doors leading to bedrooms and living rooms. The house, which is one-room deep, could be cooled by opening these doors to the breeze. If even that failed, the family could sit out on the shady porch.

These three distinct buildings hint at the wide range of architecture found on working ranches, which dotted the plains, valleys, deserts, and mountains of the West in the nineteenth and early-twentieth centuries. There was no prototype or single style seen in these ranches. They could be made of wood, stone, or adobe; one-story or two-story; formal or rustic; and they could vary by culture as well as class. If ranchers were prosperous, they might furnish their homes with the trappings of Eastern gentility—such as grand pianos, Oriental rugs, and china. John Kendrick, a wealthy Wyoming senator, owned several ranches, including one in 1890 near Hanging Woman Creek in the rolling prairie of southern Montana, which offered such comforts as an ice house. On the other end of the social scale were the basic

log dogtrots of Texas from the mid-1800s, which offered their inhabitants a breezeway as shelter from the baking sun; here, the ranch family was isolated in an often hard and difficult environment.

Some of the most comfortable and sizable ranches were the haciendas built by families awarded Spanish and Mexican land grants in California from the 1820s on. In a vast, under-populated country, these ranches became small communi-ties, almost villages, housing extended families, servants, and sometimes even a priest. Visitors were welcomed and well provided for, too. The population of the hacienda swelled and contracted as seasonal workers came and went. In California's milder climate, outdoor courtyards turned into places for domestic work, entertaining, and family life.

The materials at hand, the climate, and the needs of living usually dictated the specific nature of the ranch's prag-matic architecture, resulting in a wide range of ranch-house

Curtis Ranch, 1907, Altadena, California. Louis B. Easton, architect. Though as simple in form as the adobe Rancho Santa Margarita hacienda, Easton's wood building self-consciously reflected the aesthetic and phi-losophy of the Arts and Crafts movement; his wife, Honor, was Elbert Hubbard's sister.

Curtis Ranch, 1907, Altadena, California. Louis B. Easton, architect. Easton's structure is at the very beginning of the eventual bridging of the gap between the strictly utilitarian house on the working ranch and the suburban Ranch House invested with a philosophy. In the former, the board-and-batten structure was purely practical; however, once the Arts and Crafts philosophy bestowed the moral qualities of honesty and beauty on the same configuration of wood boards, the path was open for the suburban Ranch House, later in the century, to further infuse boards and battens (used as a veneer) with the meaning of rugged self-reliance and hospitality that had come to be associated with the Western myth.

architecture. Even rustic architecture built by untrained labor possessed an aesthetic, intended or not. The nature of the local materials endowed the structures with form, texture, and color. The no-nonsense pragmatism of ranch work imposed a direct arrangement of forms in houses, barns, stables, bunkhouses, sheds, and corrals. The abundance of land often led to a leisurely ground-hugging sprawl, while the passage of time imparted an evolutionary character seen in wings and additions as families grew and prospered.

Without effort, these utilitarian vernacular structures housing workers and animals attained a simple beauty that many twentieth-century architects could not help but admire. "The ranch house gained favor because of the sensuous appeal of its forms and materials, the reassuring massiveness of the earth walls, evident in the deep reveals of doors and windows, and the constant play of light and shadow on lightly-plastered, rude adobe brick," observed the historian Esther McCoy.[2] These were the raw structures, forms, materials, and images that contemporary architects would mine for the Ranch House style, even while they carefully edited it for modern lifestyles.

Of all the various types of historic ranch houses dotting the West, two variations proved to be the most alluring to these latter day architects: the Hispanic adobe hacienda of California—dating from as early as the 1820s and reaching a golden age in the 1840s—and the wood frame ranch building, found from the Texas plains to Northern California. One was massive and grounded in the earth; the other was a light stick-frame structure, which created crisp geometric shapes surfaced in board-and-batten or plank textures that caught the sharp sunlight. Both had a directness and simplicity that attracted architects, and a warmth of materials and historic images that attracted the public. These early ranches all provided rich fodder for the architects that created the twentieth-century Ranch House style.

Homes for the Twentieth Century

Other trends emerged at the dawn of the twentieth century that also inspired the creation of the Ranch House. At virtually the same moment, two cities—Chicago and Los Angeles—unexpectedly produced two fresh residential forms, both notably suburban. The ties to Eastern fashions of Victorian and Neo Classical architecture were looser in both cities, and the air of innovation and possibility inspired architects—including Frank Lloyd Wright, Walter Burley Griffin, George Maher, Charles Greene, and Henry Greene—to experiment, allowing new sources and a new informality of life to shape their home designs.[3] Because Chicago was far larger and better known since the 1893 Columbian Exposition, the architectural press made Wright and the Prairie Style almost immediately famous in the East and in Europe; however, it would take more than fifty years before the architectural press paid serious attention to the Greenes. But the modern seeds they planted took root and grew in the popular imagination and the commercial home-building industry.

The Prairie Style introduced a new type of residential space to American architecture. Instead of defining rooms as discrete boxes linked by doorways, Wright saw home interiors as continuous, flowing spaces. Living rooms, dining rooms, and dens could unite while maintaining their distinct functions. Likewise on the exterior, Wright rejected traditional forms for simplified ahistoric lines and ornament, and an emphatic horizontality in broad eaves, dominant hipped roofs, and Roman brick.

Wright's 1903 Prairie Style house for Edwin Cheney in suburban Oak Park, Illinois, exemplified these radical concepts. A relatively small one-story home with a broadhipped roof spreading its eaves widely over brick walls, it clung to the ground. Equally innovative was the plan that opened one room onto another in a spacious flow. Wright published a similar design in the *Ladies Home Journal* in 1901, spreading this image widely in the first decade of the century. Wright's plan would eventually help shape the Ranch House as it evolved in the 1950s.[4]

Meanwhile in California, the spirit of rebellion against conventional taste and in favor of new beginnings (the very spirit that inspired many immigrants to head West) also inspired an aesthetic reaction—the Arts and Crafts Movement, which began in England in the 1890s and 1900s before crossing the Atlantic and finding its way to the oak arroyos of Pasadena and the hills of Berkeley. In few other regions did the move-

Preludes to the Suburban Ranch House

ment take such tangible form. In these suburban areas, proponents of the Arts and Crafts movement sought a life of simplicity and closeness to nature, and a homestead of basic wood, handsomely crafted in the handwork of the past, with large windows and doors letting onto large porches.

Some Craftsman-inspired houses drew on the Mission tradition of Hispanic California with forms and plans that would later be echoed in the Ranch House. Charles and Henry Greene's rambling, one-story U-shaped plan for the 1903 Bandini House in Pasadena alluded to the California Missions and haciendas. Each room opened onto a central courtyard—an "outdoor living room" as Randell Makinson called it in *Five California Architects,* the 1960 book that reintroduced the Greene brothers to the architectural mainstream.[5] One model for the Bandini House was the Estudillo House in San Diego, a historic adobe building popularly known as "Ramona's Marriage Place." The title—which refers to the fictional heroine of Helen Hunt Jackson's 1884 novel *Ramona*—reveals the ongoing power of the media to shape popular architectural taste. This would not be the last time in the twentieth century that a literary creation would invest a style of architecture with cultural meaning; the movies would provide the same boost to the Ranch House in the 1930s, as would television in the 1950s. But in the spirit of reinvention and transformation (which the Ranch House would continue), the Greene brothers used board-

and-batten siding instead of adobe in the Bandini House; they were clearly interested not in a historic recreation, but in using vernacular forms that suited the climate and had links to the cultural landscape.[6]

Other Craftsman-style bungalows echoed the simple wood ranch houses that were also found in the agricultural San Gabriel Valley. Both made good use of simple exposed wood structures and native stonework fireplaces, and connected with the balmy Southern California climate. The Arts and Crafts movement, however, brought a new dimension to this design—a philosophy, a self-conscious meaning, was bestowed on simple rustic homes. The Arts and Crafts media (*Roycrofters* magazine, Stickley's *Craftsman* magazine published from 1901 to 1916, and others) described how these forms stood for simplicity and progressivism, for an open and healthy way of life close to nature in setting and in the very materials that sheltered the family. The Ranch House would reiterate that philosophy of simple rusticity years later—though with twentieth-century irony it would embrace the mass industrial means and methods that the Arts and Crafts movement consciously rejected.

The 1907 Curtis Ranch in Altadena by Louis B. Easton was a Craftsman-style house with the unaffected appearance of a vernacular wood stick Ranch House.[7] Easton called the Curtis ranch buildings "shacks," and like architect William Wurster twenty years later, he admired and borrowed

Left and right: Bandini House, 1903, Pasadena, California. Charles and Henry Greene, architects. Though popularly known for their work in the Craftsman style, the Greene brothers also explored other vernacular forms, such as the house situated in the U-shaped court found in California haciendas of the Spanish era. They altered the structure, however, from adobe to wood board and batten. The rustic image and the easy access between indoors and outdoors made it a predecessor of the suburban Ranch House. These characteristics would influence the young William Wurster, architect of the Gregory Farmhouse, twenty-four years later.

extensively from the conventional builder's vernacular. Instead of wood studs covered in plaster and lath, the simple gabled buildings were post-and-beam structures with true board-and-batten construction. Foot-wide redwood boards formed both the outside and inside, fixed on both sides with one-by-three battens. A porch stretched along the front of the house, its roof propped up on wood posts.

As straightforward as the Curtis Ranch appears, it was a self-consciously composed design. A builder rather than a trained architect, Louis B. Easton (1864–1921) was closely associated with the burgeoning Arts and Crafts movement in Pasadena at the time; his wife Honor was sister to Elbert Hubbard, whose 1895 Roycroft community and Roycroft Press in New York helped to define and promote the Arts and Crafts movement. Easton's client, Carl Curtis, obtained his degree in electrical engineering from Cleveland's Case Polytechnic Institute when he headed west to the San Gabriel Valley. The land inspired him to give up engineering for a more rugged outdoors life—ranching, initially chickens, but later pedigree dogs. In the citrus foothills of Altadena, he hired Easton to design a house for him. Easton's 1908 house for Laura Rinkle Johnson in Pasadena, near the Bandini House, embodies a similar shack-like simplicity, but its outdoor veranda foreshadows the lifestyle of many Ranch House owners in the 1950s; in *The Craftsman*, Johnson described the pleasures of outdoor living among exotic plants, shady oaks, and reflecting pools.[8]

The best known Craftsman-style homes, however, are the grand homes designed by Charles and Henry Greene, such as the 1908 house for the wealthy Gamble family in Pasadena. Here the bungalow rose to an exquisite and unique architecture. Built of wood, in the face of the prevailing Spanish stucco taste, and Orientalist in ornament compared to the classical leaves and volutes of Victorian architecture, the house's rooms were large and spacious, with terraces that united the living spaces, and sleeping porches that opened the private areas to the air, views, and sky. The high-style bungalows in the Craftsman style were artfully contradictory designs: by exposing their sinewy wood beam structures, they seemed boldly informal in an age of Victorian architecture that hid structure beneath opulent ornament; yet the

Greene brothers' exposed beams and posts were exquisitely carved and polished. This adroit glorification of simplicity—supported by the Arts and Crafts philosophy and literature which praised honest and plain living—would make the Craftsman-style bungalow widely popular.

Homes Times One Hundred

When the Gambles and other wealthy families embraced the simple rustic wood structures of the Craftsman-style bungalow, the style was made acceptable—even fashionable—for the middle classes. This would not be the last time in the twentieth century that an upper-class style was democratized and repackaged for the middle class—and even the working class.[9]

Coinciding with this creation of an architectural fashion came the means and methods for spreading it through the consumer culture. At the same time that the Greene brothers were building, other Pasadena architects, such as Sylvanus Marston and Arthur Heineman, were reshaping and downsizing the bungalow into small cottages for vacationers, as well as for middle-class and working-class families. Though the Craftsman-style bungalow shrank in size, it retained its aesthetic. In the work of the Greene brothers, the exposed post-and-beam structures had been exquisitely and expensively crafted, showing off the metal-strapped connections and the masterfully carved rafter ends. But even in more modest examples, the structure was made integrally ornamental: exposed rafters created a decorative rhythm around the eave line; a wide-eave, gently pitched roof hid the volume of the house in its shadows, creating a compelling image of shelter. Plain, unpainted redwood ceiling beams and shingles, and malformed clinker brick were imbued with a philosophical purpose.

The building industry geared itself to take advantage of the public's interest in the bungalow. At the dawn of the twentieth century—as movies were being born in New Jersey and California, as William Randolph Hearst and Joseph Pulitzer were inventing the modern mass media, and as Henry Ford was preparing to put the nation on wheels—the building industry was preparing for its role in the mass culture to come. Companies such as the Bungalow

Preludes to the Suburban Ranch House

Building Company in Seattle, Bungalowcraft, The Pacific Building Company, and Southern California Standard Building Investment Company in Los Angeles, sold lots, built bungalow houses, and offered loans and insurance for the average home buyer.[10] Both Sears, Roebuck & Co., and Montgomery Ward offered prefab houses. Homemaking magazines promoted bungalows, which also appeared in plan books that allowed would-be homeowners to select a plan and a size of house, take it to a local home contractor, and have their dream house built. In these forms, the bungalow rapidly spread once it caught fire in the popular imagination, just as the Ranch House would do forty years later.[11]

The popularity of the bungalow, however, fostered another form of housing development: the bungalow court. A typical example was Sylvanus B. Marston's 1909 St. Francis Court, a community of eleven small bungalows intended for the use of vacationers to Pasadena, and developed by the Frank G. Hogan Company. Situated on a cul-de-sac street to allow arrival by car (though no garages were included), the unpainted wood frame cottages reflected the Craftsman style. Each of the eleven was slightly different in design and plan, but together they created a planned streetscape that balanced unity with individuality.[12] Each bungalow-court house was built individually, not by the mass assembly-line techniques that would be developed in the late 1930s. Yet, grouped into a small neighborhood of affordable homes, and unified by landscaped grounds and walkways, bungalow courts were early, primitive forerunners of future mass tract developments that would spread over the San Gabriel Valley and throughout the Los Angeles metropolitan area in the 1950s.

As the spiritual father of the bungalow, however, Charles Greene decried the idea of mass production, even in such an agreeable form as the bungalow court. "The perfect bungalow should be designed to fit the needs of a particular owner. A house built to sell is like a slop-shop coat; it will cover most any man's back but a gentleman's, unless misfortune preclude a choice. . . . the bungalow court idea is to be regretted. Born of the ever-present speculator, it not only has the tendency to increase unnecessarily the cost of the land, but it never admits of home building. It

must either be a renting or buying proposition."[13] Thus, at the very beginning of the twentieth century, the bungalow and its rising popularity set up the conflict of custom design versus mass-produced housing, a controversy to be faced again by the Ranch House in the 1950s. However, mass production, as the wave of the future, was already winning. The twentieth century would nurture forces and trends that could not sustain Charles Greene's gentlemanly approach to design. The speculator and the developer would formulate the means to house the masses in ways the Arts and Crafts generation did not imagine. But the Craftsman-style bungalow's gentle image of the rustic and simple lifestyle on the land would survive—albeit in altered forms.

The Ranch House's Essence

There was yet another predecessor that demonstrated the alchemical blend of place and climate, of a vernacular history and a modern building system, that was to come to full fruitage in the popular Ranch House of the 1950s. R. M. Schindler's 1921 house on Kings Road in Los Angeles continued Southern California's architectural experiments with outdoor living, already seen in the Craftsman-style bungalows. Like Henry Greene's 1903 Bandini House and Wurster's 1927 Gregory Farmhouse, the Kings Road House is an example of a California architect transforming the possibilities of vernacular architecture.

In 1915, Schindler rode the train from Chicago through New Mexico and Arizona to California. On the way he stopped and studied the adobe architecture of New Mexico. His interest in the architecture is seen in the unbuilt Taos house he designed that same year for Dr. T. P. Martin. Incorporating the region's traditional courtyard plan, this Austrian-trained Modernist in Pueblo country unashamedly blended past and present in a manner that he repeated, in a more sophisticated manner, in his own house six years later. The battered adobe walls of the Martin design transfigured into the progressive concrete tilt-up construction, but the solid earthen textures and sloped walls remained, tying the house to the ground. The tilt-up concrete walls—already used successfully by Irving Gill, whose Dodge House (1914) stood across the street—was a building technique that could

Preludes to the Suburban Ranch House

be applied in mass production. Learning from Frank Lloyd Wright, Schindler experimented with new living styles and open plans, and with single spaces embracing several functions. Above all, the architect created patios with outdoor fireplaces—where living could be carried on in the benign Southern California climate; sliding wood-and-canvas panels and glass walls allowed the sheltered interiors to flow into the outdoors, an early application of the sliding-glass doors that became an identifying feature in the Ranch House thirty years later. In significant ways, the Kings Road House was a prototype, in spirit, of the revolution in mass housing that the Ranch House represented. Tract developers used other materials, and their plans were different in configuration. But the Kings Road House is a precursor because it grasped that home design could respond to new lifestyles and environments in the West. In throwing off the past, it created a new architecture.

Neither the Kings Road House, the Craftsman-style bungalow, nor the Prairie Style house are direct predecessors of the Ranch House as it would develop in the 1930s. But they laid the foundations for new themes in residential architecture—themes related to informal living, indoor-outdoor spaces, rustic aesthetics and natural materials, simple construction simply expressed, a low profile, a fascination with the vernacular (particularly the working ranch

house of the nineteenth century), and most significantly mass-produced housing—which the Ranch House continued.

Historians often identify Cliff May as "the first designer to revive the Ranch House" in the 1930s, but in many ways the Ranch House never truly disappeared.[14] The hacienda plan—with outdoor and indoor spaces overlapping—showed up in the Greene's 1903 Bandini House, Henry Greene's 1913 Crowe House, Schindler's 1921 Kings Road House, Roland Coate's 1925 James K. Tweedy House in Downey, California, in the car court of Wurster's 1927 Gregory Farmhouse, as well as May's first speculative houses in 1932.[15] The low, ground-hugging profile and rustic wood structures of the Bandini, Curtis Ranch, and numerous Craftsman-style and vernacular buildings were constants in the architectural landscape. Henry H. Saylor, editor of *The American Architect* (and a promoter of the bungalow), already recognized the Ranch House as an architectural type in 1925.[16] The bungalow court and prefab houses began testing out ways to build not just one custom house, but efficient multiple houses. In these examples, Modern concepts were already being blended with historical imagery of plain ranches in a new house type. Biding its time, working its way into the popular consciousness in the West, the Ranch House blossomed in a thousand examples once the economic and cultural climate was ready in the 1950s.

Gregory Farmhouse, 1927, Scotts Valley, California. William Wurster, architect. Stockton-native Wurster knew and admired the simple vernacular buildings of central California (most were of wood construction and rurally sited). At a time when avant-garde Modern architecture was self-consciously injecting sleek Machine-Age imagery into architecture, Wurster was instead inspired by those crude but powerful wood structures he had grown up with— an example of the "trickle up" phenomenon in which high-art design was influenced by untutored but good design. The Gregory Farmhouse looks, at first glance, like nothing so much as a collection of sheds. Yet Wurster rendered their artless wood structures with a sophisticated rusticity of elegant proportions and minimal details. The Ranch image, long present in the American consciousness, was becoming high art.

Before the Boom: The Invention of the Suburban Ranch House

The Ranch House was the home of the American twentieth century. Breaking with traditional styles and building methods, it emerged from an amalgam of mid-century trends: governmental housing policy encouraging home ownership, Hollywood Westerns spreading the magnetic myth and images of rugged individualism, new technologies (from electric saws to automatic dishwashers) reshaping the American house, and increasingly casual lifestyles creating a need for informal house plans. With the introduction of modern architectural ideas and growing prosperity, enormous numbers of blue-collar workers were able to join the middle-class suburban lifestyle.

Ranch homes existed before this twentieth-century incarnation—in California's haciendas, Texas dogtrots, and Montana log cabins. They also existed as an ideal image in cowboy novels and movies. But few of these examples looked entirely like the Ranch House as it would blossom in hundreds of suburbs in the mid-twentieth century. That type had to be invented.

The cover of *Sunset* magazine in July 1930 featured the new Ranch-style home that architect William Wurster designed in 1927 above Santa Cruz for Sadie Gregory, a recently widowed San Francisco Bay Area woman. It was called a farmhouse, but the magazine presented it to look like the set for a Western movie: simple four-by-four posts held up the long straight wood-roofed porch of a bunk house. A cowboy and cowgirl couple, he in chaps, she in Tom Mix hat, stood in the foreground, heightening the impression that this was an authentic piece of Western life, even though the house was brand new.

That Western myth was proving to be an enduring commodity. Brochures for the 1942 Ranch-style Last Frontier Hotel in Las Vegas ("the Early West in Modern Splendor") featured cowboys and cowgirls sitting on split rail fences;

architect-owner William Moore had moved historic buildings from Nevada mining towns to create a small tourist attraction behind his hotel and casino. A decade later Walter Knott did the same at his chicken and boysenberry pie restaurant in Buena Park, and a decade later Walt Disney fashioned his own Old West town at Disneyland's Frontierland. The 1954 brochure for the tract homes at Lakewood Rancho Estates (designed by Cliff May and Chris Choate) featured a modern cowboy and cowgirl couple in denim, ten-gallon hats, and pearl button shirts.

Popular culture was brimming with the myth of the West in the 1930s and 1940s. A folk song with a verse about a home where the buffalo roam had been picked out of an obscure anthology and turned into an American icon. Aaron Copland composed the cowboy ballets *Billy the Kid* (1938) and *Rodeo* (1942). In the 1940s and 1950s, Bob Wills and his Texas Playboys brought their jumping mix of jazz and Western music from Oklahoma City and Turkey, Texas, to a Californian constituency in Fresno, Visalia, Modesto, and Los Angeles. In 1939, Country and Western singer Gene Autry sang the cowboy-themed "Back in the Saddle Again" and moved into the mainstream of popular culture; in 1943, Bing Crosby invoked a metaphorical West in his song "San Fernando Valley," which was then still a valley full of ranches, including the spreads of actors Raymond Griffith (designed by Lloyd Wright), Joel McCrea, and Clark Gable. The West served a national purpose as a myth long after it served as a place for settlement.[1] The appeal of the ranch in the movies—mythic home, buckaroo Valhalla of celluloid heroes like John Wayne, Gary Cooper, Roy Rogers, and Gene Autry—indirectly prepared the market for Ranch House buyers.[2]

A surge of nativism, encouraged by the reconstruction of Colonial Williamsburg and of Franciscan Mission churches in California in the 1920s and 1930s, extended naturally to

House, c. 1850, New Braunfels, Texas. This and scores of other homes designed in the Texan vernacular were photographed by architect David R. Williams in the early twentieth century. Like Wurster, who also found value in vernacular traditions, Williams was attracted to the simple forms of the region, forms that reflected regional materials, climate, history, and character, at a time when America was embracing a revival of American Colonial and various European styles of architecture.

ranches and mining towns. Scholarship supported these cultural narratives; the Historic American Buildings Survey, founded in 1933 under the National Park Service, hired unemployed architects to document historic buildings nationwide. The dispersion of architects into the hinterlands and the resulting gush of drawings spotlighted an underappreciated resource. Many architects were captivated by the solid, modest, functional vernacular structures they discovered for themselves, and many drew on these buildings for their own architecture.

The Lure of the Vernacular
Among the architects intrigued with buildings of the rural West were Californian Wurster (1895-1973) and Texan O'Neil Ford (1905-1982). Born in Stockton, Wurster had long been acquainted with the simple wood ranch buildings of central California; with his mentor and colleague David Reichard Williams (1890-1962), Ford had traveled hundreds of miles through small Texas towns photographing and sketching the stone and wood homes of nineteenth-century pioneers. Of course, the urbane Wurster, who recently graduated from the

School of Architecture at the University of California, and his client Sadie Gregory were not Western hicks. With a degree from the University of Chicago (where she had studied with Thorstein Veblen, author of *The Theory of the Leisure Class*), Mrs. Gregory and her friends—many of whom became Wurster's clients—had no pretensions about being cowboys. They simply wished to have country homes near enough to San Francisco or Berkeley that would blend with the rural landscape of Northern California's coastal mountains.[3]

At a glance, the Gregory Farmhouse appears as a collection of ordinary vernacular ranch buildings around a court.[4] However, as in most Wurster designs, appearances are deceiving; the details, composition, and craftsmanship belie the rusticity. A tower reminiscent of local water towers stood at the entry. A covered outdoor porch faced the court, and was a main link between the many rooms. The plank interior walls had minimal trim detailing and added a subtle texture. The studied placement of windows filled the rooms with balanced light and each room had a private outdoor space. In historian Marc Treib's words, it was an architecture of "sophisticated rusticity."[5] "Wurster sought to authenticate his early houses by employing an aesthetic of ordinariness—and, at times, a seemingly deliberate awkwardness—to at once qualify their historicity and mitigate a too easy accessibility," wrote Howard Barnstone, the biographer of Wurster's contemporary John Staub.[6] Wurster himself described the farmhouse as "a house of carpenter architecture—no wood beams or posts larger than absolutely necessary—an arid, California yard with the protecting walls about."[7]

"The Depression itself played an important role in promoting the studied lack of ostentation that became a Wurster hallmark," notes historian Dan Gregory, grandson of Wurster's client. "This was because economic reality made it almost impossible to build in the traditional architectural styles that were so labor-intensive and dependent on richness of detail for their effects. In other words, simplicity became a necessity if one were to build at all. Unlike a less original architect, however, who might have tried to produce the appearance of traditional architecture on a smaller budget, Wurster seized upon the concept of simplicity and made it into a conscious esthetic."[8]

As an example of the emerging regional Modernism mixing vernacular traditions with modern concepts and forms, the Gregory Farmhouse would boost Wurster's career. It would also help spread the image of the Ranch House to the popular audiences of *Sunset* and *House Beautiful*. Wurster would go on to become a major figure in the architecture profession—he was dean of the architecture schools at the University of California and then the Massachusetts Institute of Technology, and he ran a large commercial firm, Wurster Bernardi and Emmons, in San Francisco. He and his partners also designed custom houses, ranging from elegant San Francisco townhouses to formal Atherton mansions. But Ranch Houses continued to be a consistent part of his residential designs into the 1950s. The 1932 Gallway House in Pasatiempo, like the Gregory Farmhouse, takes the form of a collection of ranch sheds, but is even more strikingly rustic with its wood plank walls finished in a worn and weathered finish.[9] The 1939 Gwerder House in Walnut Grove is based on a different vernacular type—the rectangular, wood frame Ranch House with a single gable and porch stretching along the entire front of the house.

Though Wurster, according to his biographer Richard Peters, did not use the term "Ranch" as an identifying label for these houses, historians such as David Gebhard, Esther McCoy, and others have since applied the term to many Wurster designs; as Gebhard wrote, they were "lightly modernized California ranch houses."[10]

A similar direct translation of a vernacular Ranch House form could be seen two years after the Gregory Farmhouse in the studio O'Neil Ford (an admirer and later a friend of Wurster) designed for the artist Jerry Bywaters in a Dallas suburb. O'Neil Ford was as much an artifact of the Texas soil as the historic buildings of East Texas that he admired. His architectural training came through courses at the International Correspondence Schools and then working with David Williams (who also took courses with ICS). By all reports a cantankerous, colorful, larger-than-life character, Ford parlayed his small-town-boy persona into a major presence in national architectural circles.

In contrast to the massive, formal Romanesque, Classical Revival, and Second Empire civic buildings of Sherman, Texas,

on the Oklahoma border—where Ford grew up and attended North Texas State Teachers College in Denton—the simple geometries and unornamented walls of the small homes he saw on his automobile tours appeared strikingly fresh. On one three-week car trip through Central Texas with his brother Lynn, the pair took over six hundred photos of old buildings with a cheap box camera.[11] As Williams wrote, "It is better to throw away our habit of supposing everything beautiful in Texas has a foreign origin, and to admit that these little houses are not French or Spanish or even English at all, but are natural, native Texas art, suited to our climate and indigenous to our soil. We should be very proud of them. We should use them as sources from which to draw a beautiful architecture which we could call our own and then invite the world to come and see."[12]

Ford's design emerged directly from his observations of vernacular Ranch buildings. Around the time that folklorist John Avery Lomax (another Texan and a friend of Williams) was traveling the south recording blues and folk singers in the late 1920s and early 1930s, Ford and Williams were driving the back roads of Texas in a big second-hand Packard Straight Eight open touring car. As they drove through small towns—including Castroville, Fredericksburg, Brackettville, New Braunfels, and Roma and San Ygnacio along the Rio Grande—they would photograph and sketch this architectural history and living textbook.[13]

Mid-nineteenth century immigrants from France, Germany, Poland, Spain, and elsewhere brought their European building precedents and adapted them to the local materials (porous limestone of the San Antonio region for thick walls, clay adobe of the El Paso region) and the harsh summer heat to develop a vernacular Ranch House architecture.[14] These designs retained some Alsatian and French conventions, placing the houses right on the street, with the back of the house opening onto a private rear yard for gardens and flowers. The homes were often simple steep-gabled boxes with minimal eaves, often with a covered porch along the front. Metal roofs were common, as were shutters, screen doors, and large chimneys. As Williams noted, these houses, "seemed to grow out of the land on which they stood; and they were beautiful because they were simple and natural, and because their builders were honest enough to be satisfied with beauty of line, and simplicity and delicacy of details."[15]

Jerry Bywaters later said of the studio Ford designed for him, "I didn't realize until years later that my studio was almost a dead ringer for a little house next door to the bakery in downtown New Braunfels . . . a nice little one-story house with a steep pitched roof."[16] That building (the Klein-Naegelin House, c. 1846), is a simple *fachwerk* structure with a steep pitched roof. Ford appropriated the steep gable almost exactly, but instead of its wood frame structure in-filled with stone and stucco, he substituted brick. He also cleaned up the details of the original building, which were crude and worn with time; it was not the patina that interested Ford (as it would a Ranch House architect such as Cliff May), but the forms and the plan, including the porch. With such explorations of form, detail, and images, the homely Ranch House was ready to join the Colonial, the Tudor, and the French Regency as the preferred style for custom home architects across the nation.

Ranch House Neighborhoods

Around the same time that the modern suburban Ranch House was being formally designed, the first neighborhoods using the style also emerged. The Ranch was no longer a solitary structure set in splendid isolation on the prairie; though not yet mass produced as they would be in the 1940s and 1950s, the custom Ranch Houses of Rolling Hills took some of the first steps to creating a workable urban/suburban community.

A. E. Hanson was the General Manager of the Palos Verdes Corporation, the development company which turned part of the Palos Verdes peninsula into an exclusive home development in 1922.[17] There, steep cliffs overlooking an azure sea enhanced the Mediterranean setting that Charles Cheney, Myron Hunt, and the sons of Frederick Law Olmsted exploited in the development of Palos Verdes. There they had planted, graded, and designed the site as a haven of posh Spanish- and Andalusian-style homes, centered on a Spanish Village town center.

The remainder of the Palos Verdes peninsula was an almost treeless rolling landscape used for cattle grazing.

Though attached to the alluvial plain of the Los Angeles basin, the peninsula is ecologically and geologically similar to the dramatic offshore islands of Santa Catalina and San Clemente. Here, in 1932, Hanson planned a development that offered a completely different image and scene than the Iberian Palos Verdes Estates. Los Angeles, many have noted, has little indigenous historical architecture beyond the missions and Chumash huts. Thus, in the 1920s, the streets of Beverly Hills, Culver City, and Hollywood blossomed with a thousand images, a thousand themes, and thousands of houses: miniature Tudor mansions, fairy tale cottages, Southern plantation houses, and Egyptian bungalow courts. In contrast, at Palos Verdes Estates, the theming was extended to an entire development, an entire landscape. And so, next to Andalusia, Hanson decided to build the Old West. Rolling Hills would be Ranch themed.

"Own your own dude ranch—not for profit, but for pleasure," enticed the sales brochures of 1932. Upper-middle class families in Los Angeles were offered a second home, a virtual vacation home, only a short drive but an entire world away from the city. Part of Hanson's inspiration was a lifestyle-marketing concept: large lots with enough space to allow for small stables; a necklace of bridal trails strung through the eucalyptus, stretching over grassy hillsides, through wooded ravines, and along crestlines with breathtaking ocean vistas. Hanson's Ranch theme was also inspired by an existing house—an authentic vernacular building built sometime between 1885 and 1890 for the working ranchers tending the grazing cattle. It was a small gabled wood frame structure with board-and-batten walls, and tongue-and-groove paneling inside. Hanson first made it his family's home; when they stretched its capacity by staking out tents, it was dubbed "Rancho Elastico." In 1933, it became a model home to promote sales of lots in the development initially called Rancho Palos Verdes.

As Charles Cheney wrote in May 1935, "At mile three is Rolling Hills where five- to ten-acre 'Dude ranches' offer ideal outdoor life, seclusion, privacy, recreation, horseback riding, cultivation of friends and vegetables, and the enjoyment of a country atmosphere, all protected by good restrictions."[18] But at the dark dawn of the Great

Depression, sales dragged. Hanson later believed that the site was too near to town to sell as vacation homes, so he recast Rolling Hills as a full-time community. Instead of horse ranches, lots were one to five acres, though they retained the riding trails and stables. The main thoroughfare, Palos Verdes Drive, was 200-feet wide, stretching from Portuguese Bend Road up the hill to the ridge, with ranch gates at the entry.

For their Ranch Houses, the wealthy lot buyers often hired the notable Los Angeles architects who designed their Beverly Hills or San Marino homes, including Sumner Spaulding, Paul R. Williams, and Lutah Maria Riggs (see p. 86). Skilled at various historic styles, they designed rustic—though comfortable—Ranches that kept within the strict design guidelines of Rolling Hills. Outdoor living terraces were common features.

Palos Verdes Drive winds along a ravine, revealing glimpses of Ranch homes on distant ridges and hillsides, picturesquely framed by eucalyptus boughs and pyracantha bushes. White corral fences and small stables vary the view of houses with white board-and-batten siding and shingled roofs. The town is distinctly suburban in plan, though rural in image; the landscape is recreational and residential, not rural and industrial as were the traditional working ranches. This layout inspired most later Ranch House tracts in evoking the wide open spaces and the isolation of rugged individualism while achieving suburban densities—a balance that would suit conditions of the mid-twentieth century city. Fiercely defending its Ranch-design guidelines, Rolling Hills maintained a spacious, idealized Ranch House landscape—an idyll that scores of mass-produced subdivisions later sought to emulate.[19]

Rolling Hills was not the only Ranch-style community developed in the early 1930s. Though much smaller, Smoke Tree Ranch in Palm Springs was begun as a private enclave of vacation homes in 1929, adopting a Ranch theme to emphasize a rustic equestrian lifestyle. This theme was enforced by design guidelines; some lots were held in common view to maintain the feel of the open desert; native flora was retained; families ate at a common dining hall; and all architectural styles were controlled. Even the well-

known local Modernists Albert Frey and William Cody (who designed a home for the Walt Disney family) kept convincingly to the Ranch style.

The federal government also turned to the Ranch House for Depression-era public projects. In 1931, in Boulder City, Nevada, one-story wood or brick Ranch houses had one of their first mass-produced applications in a planned community to house the workers and administrators building Hoover Dam. In 1936, the Farm Security Administration in El Monte, east of Los Angeles, built small Ranch homes designed by architect Joseph Weston.[20] The Ranch House as an architectural type and the Ranch House tract as a planned community were developing simultaneously.

The Impact of Outsiders

The evolution of the Ranch House depended to a significant degree on architects outside the professional mainstream, who explored the romanticism of the vernacular house on a working ranch. The architect most identified with this style was Cliff May, a San Diego band leader and furniture designer who had no architectural training when he designed his first Ranch House in 1931. Another architect known for this style

House, c. 1850, Fredericksburg, Texas. Texas architect David R. Williams' camera lens shows us exactly what caught his architect's eye as he drove the back roads of Texas searching for architectural inspiration. Vernacular architecture of the American West, shaped by culture, history, and site, proved a richer source for Williams and most of the architects who helped shaped the Ranch House.

Elbert Williams House, 1932, Dallas, Texas. David R. Williams, architect. The forms that Williams borrowed from the Texan vernacular are obvious, from the metal gabled roof to the porches. The informal composition also echoes the character of houses on working ranches, many of which gained additions through the years as families grew and prospered.

was Texan David Williams, who—unlike most Western architects who had the opportunity to move to New York or study in Europe—never rejected his provincial roots. Williams studied architecture in Paris in the early 1920s; he drove through the Loire Valley admiring the architecture as he had done through East Texas; and he lived a Bohemian life in Greenwich Village before returning to Dallas in 1923 to establish an architecture practice passionately based on native Texas architecture.[21]

The Elbert Williams House (1932) in Dallas was a direct response to the houses he and O'Neil Ford saw on their backroads tours. Described as "a Rambling Texas Home" and as an "urbanized Ranch" house, it had the direct and simple forms of vernacular rural buildings in Texas—notably different than those in California.[22] It was two stories, with a porch on the second floor, with similar features to those seen in the Monterey Revival-style house. The main volume in brick is topped with a standing-seam copper roof; a secondary wing suggesting a slightly smaller addition extends off of it, with a third one-story wing off of that. Williams, who filled his houses with hand-crafted paneling, stairwells, and cabinets,

repeated specific Western-themed elements in the Lone Star motif throughout the house—a mural of Spanish missions over a fireplace, cowhide sofas, and bunk beds in the children's rooms. Newel posts and open stair railings were vernacular elements rendered luxurious by Williams's craftsmen for an upscale home. Similar to Cliff May's and Wurster's designs around the same time, the rooms were still defined as boxes, with no attempt to create open plans. However, Williams's houses included porches with French doors off most rooms; the connection to the outside was just as important in these Ranch houses as any in the 1950s. In adapting a rustic vernacular to a refined upper-middle class home, Williams put himself in league with Wurster.

On the backroads of Texas, Williams had discovered the source for developing an indigenous Texan architecture. He and O'Neil Ford promoted the idea in magazines such as the *Southwest Review*, and lectured on the concept of a regional architecture at a time when Houston and Dallas millionaires preferred the stately historical-revival homes of architects such as John Staub. In the houses they designed, they explored the connections between native ranch houses and contemporary forms, but often they met with resistance. In 1930, when Williams submitted a design in the indigenous style to a magazine for publication, the reply came "What style is it? It's got to be in some style we can recognize."[23] Williams later wrote: "In the many beautiful little houses left scattered over Texas by early settlers there is full proof that some of our grandfathers and most of our great-grandfathers possessed the refined taste and culture for which we have been searching abroad. They were not to be bound down by tradition; so they began building, not as they had built in England or France or Germany, but to suit their own needs and to satisfy as best they could the exactions of climate and the limitations of the natural materials to be found close at hand."[24]

From his observations of vernacular working-ranch houses, Williams noted the placement of porches, verandas, and wings in relation to the sun, and the use of screened sleeping porches and shaded patios. The large flat planes of whitewashed walls seen in the indigenous designs found their way into his home designs. Standing-seam metal roofs and simplified ornament were also borrowed. "Here are nicely moulded casings, a carefully proportioned porch cornice, and delicately moulded door," he noted in a San Antonio example.[25]

The Elbert Williams House was also to be Williams's last house design as the Depression took its toll on his potential clients. In 1933, he took a job with the Federal Government which ended his architectural exploration—though not his interest—in the ranch vernacular of Texas.[26] By the mid-1930s, national interest in regional architecture was growing, boosted in Texas by the 1936 Centennial. Williams's work began to garner recognition. The Elbert Williams House was published in *Better Homes and Gardens* in June 1937 in an article titled "The Ranch-House Goes to Town." But Williams later wrote, "I'd never called my Texas houses 'ranch.'"[27] Clearly, the term's definition was still unsettled, given one distinct identity by real-estate ads, brochures, and magazines, but not fully embraced as a label by the high-art architects who employed it.

Meanwhile, O'Neil Ford carried on designing homes. His Texas Ranch Houses following the Bywaters Studio are more similar to Williams's Elbert Williams House, on which Ford also worked. His Ranches are often two story, with overhanging balconies. But as seen in the two-story 1942 Murchison House in San Antonio, the horizontal lines dominate, as do the sprawling wings reaching into the landscape. These houses are plainly not Georgian or any other historic style; rather, their simplicity of form and ornament show the influence of the Texas vernacular.

Cliff May was another designer outside the mainstream who grew up around the nineteenth-century working-ranch house and later drew them into his work. "Home Designer Perfected the Ranch Style," stated his obituary in the *Los Angeles Times* on October 20, 1989, a judgment testifying more to his unstinting promotion of the Ranch style in magazines and books than to his actual invention of the type. In his "Cliff May Homes" he plunged successfully into the mass-produced housing field with his partner Chris Choate, building sizable tracts from Cupertino to Houston.

May designed his first house in San Diego in 1931, and by the time he developed the Riviera Ranch subdivision in 1939, the Ranch House had already been mastered by many archi-tects as an architectural form and style. But May's promotion of the Ranch style contributed substantially to the evolution and popularization of the twentieth-century suburban Ranch House. Namely, he influenced the mass-audience magazines, which shaped and reflected the public taste among tens of thousands of middle-class home buyers—the taste to which mass-housing developers eventually responded.

Born in San Diego, May lead a jazz dance orchestra while in school. By 1930, before completing college, he was designing and building Arts and Crafts- and Mission-style furniture. Realizing in the early 1930s that presenting his creations in a suitable setting would help sales, he displayed his furniture in his future father-in-law's model homes. In 1931, success inspired him to design his first house (for Colonel and Mrs. Arthur J. O'Leary) working with grading contractor O. U. Miracle.[28] A low-slung home with stucco walls and Spanish-tile roof, it was an unstartling version of the Spanish style familiar in Southern California at this time. As a sixth generation Californian, May drew on his own and his family's memories of the old ranchos and haciendas of Southern California (his relatives owned Rancho Santa Margarita y Las Flores, now Camp Pendleton near Oceanside); yet May also grew up across the street from a house designed by Irving Gill, an early explorer of the materials and forms of Modernism.

Between 1931 and 1937, May built fifty custom and speculative Ranch-style homes in the San Diego area. May's early advertisements promoted the authenticity and care of his details; he consciously used materials that showed off a hand-hewn or handcrafted character; though the houses were conventional wood frame construction, May made every effort to convey the look of adobe. The ads also assured potential customers that authenticity did not reduce the house's modern comforts; May's houses were never historical recreations, but historic evocations, with all the comforts of modern living.[29]

In 1934, May was commissioned by John A. Smith, a Los Angeles oil man, to design a house in La Habra Heights in eastern Los Angeles County. At Smith's urging, May shifted his Ranch building business to Los Angeles. It was a good move; not only were there more wealthy potential clients, as a media center, Los Angeles was also a better platform

to promote his Ranch House concept. While Wurster focused on the abstract simplicity of working-ranch structures, May gloried in its picturesque qualities. The 1935 Lilypond House in Mandeville Canyon is typical of his early designs (see p. 82). Moderate in size, the house has a stucco wall facing the street and a breezeway behind a gate that leads to the front door and an inner courtyard. The superb use of the lot creates different outdoor areas on different sides, which are easily accessed and expand the apparent size of the house. A picture window framed in wide horizontal panes connects the living room to the court; only later did May use sliding doors to create the same effect. Details perfect May's picture: adobe texturing is trowelled over the wood frame structure; wood grills protect windows; exposed beams form the ceiling of the living room.

At the Riviera Ranch development in 1939, May created a small planned subdivision of custom homes (see p. 92). Extending up Sullivan Canyon in a landscape of steep cliffs and lush vegetation worthy of a Western movie setting, and located just off Sunset Boulevard when Brentwood was still far from the city, Riviera Ranch offered horse properties adjacent to the mountain trails. A corral and riding ring were provided for the community on the site of a school that was never built; in 1939 stables stood in the flat land across Sunset. In these houses the themes of his hallmark Ranch houses emerged as he selected or rejected historic elements from the haciendas. Like Charles and Henry Greene and Frederick Louis Roehrig (among others), who adapted the hacienda form to their designs thirty years before, May's divergences from the historic type are as informative as the similarities.

May's conceit, he claimed, was that he was designing what the Californios, the gregarious Europeans who settled California, would have built if they lived in 1946.[30] The outdoor *corredor* colonnade became enclosed as the house's major circulation path. Where U-shaped haciendas were emphatically rectilinear, May splayed the wings to widen the views from rooms, create an expansive patio, and emphasize the self-consciously casual character of the houses. In place of the rigid social hierarchy of the haciendas, May invented an informal plan for a new lifestyle.[31]

With several irregular wings sprawling over the site, a Cliff May Ranch House can easily be expanded without disturbing the congenial, informal rambling character of the house. Conventional Modernism would have accommodated expansion with a rationalized module based on a structural system, adding on similar modules on a Cartesian grid. May accomplished the same flexibility and unified appearance using a picturesque form. Indeed, his custom homes have the air of a movie set; he focused carefully on stucco textures, hand-carved wood, corner fireplaces, and other beguiling details to set the tone of a house.[32] Exposed wood beam ceilings and trusses revealed the structure and added appealing warmth. Front doors were close-ups for a kind of welcoming agrarian homestead, like the opening scene for a movie about a noble family of the land. Hand-carved doors hinted at a cherishing of the past and benchlike pot shelves running along the base provided splashes of Technicolor geraniums which set the scene in a benign climate.

Inside, the viewer's eye is drawn through widescreen picture windows to the expansive and meticulously landscaped backyard. Concrete slab floors, often at the same level as the ground, smoothly unite the indoors with the outdoors. There is often no step or sill. The kitchens are informal, sunny, and rustic, radiating hospitality and sized for convivial gatherings of friends and family. The bedrooms are havens, equipped with their own private courtyards.

The narrative May created in his custom houses was not a formal architectural concept taught at any architecture school. May's status as a house *designer*—he was not a registered architect—apparently allowed him to sense and develop this novel aspect of architecture in the twentieth century. Wurster's Gregory Farmhouse Ranch design was the first on *Sunset's* cover, but while Wurster went on to design a variety of building types, May devoted his career primarily to the Ranch House.

The Contemporary Ranch House Emerges
O'Neil Ford, David Williams, Cliff May, and William Wurster approached the Ranch House from their love of the vernacular, and then updated the type with modernized plans, aesthetics, and structural concepts.[33] Harwell Hamilton

Before the Boom

Harris (1903-1990) approached the issue of the one-story single family suburban house from the standpoint of the Modernist camp. Harris learned European Modernism at the best place a young architect could hope to in California in the late 1920s, working in the office of Richard Neutra. Harris was born amid the citrus orchards of the Inland Empire in Redlands, California, and raised on a 160-acre ranch in the rich Imperial Valley. He studied design at Otis Institute in Los Angeles and did not visit New York until 1940. He watched the construction of Neutra's magnificent steel-frame Lovell Health House firsthand; he also experienced urbanism in the middle of the emerging suburban metropolis of Los Angeles. It is no wonder, then, that (in the estimation of Kenneth Frampton) Harris "sought to render the American suburb as a place of culture."[34] His houses were solidly suburban in planning and sensibility.

Harris was steeped in the fertile environment of modern architecture that developed in California long before the Bauhaus was founded. The Craftsman-style bungalows of Pasadena were familiar to him, though he did not know of Charles and Henry Sumner Greene—no one did—until the 1940s; his wife Jean Murray Bangs was one of the first historians to recognize their work. He was captivated early on by Frank Lloyd Wright's original forms and inventions, and the spatial character of a house as a part of nature. He had a friend at Otis Institute, Ruth Sowden, whose family had selected Lloyd Wright to design their 1927 house in Los Feliz, a house which threw open the doors and walls of every room to a lush outdoor courtyard. He visited R. M. Schindler's house on Kings Road, another proto-Ranch home of spaciousness and ease; in his own design sensibility, Harris was closer to Schindler than to Neutra. While Neutra brought his ideas from Europe, Harris pointedly embraced the potent, youthful culture he found in Los Angeles. Harris's background fostered his interest in the local wood tradition, in houses that blended with nature, and in the single-family suburban home, rather than European workers' housing. Such were his contributions to the Ranch House.

Harris's 1933 house for Pauline Lowe and Clive Delbridge in Altadena sat under a wide-eave hipped roof. Though the design reflects many influences (including Japanese archi-

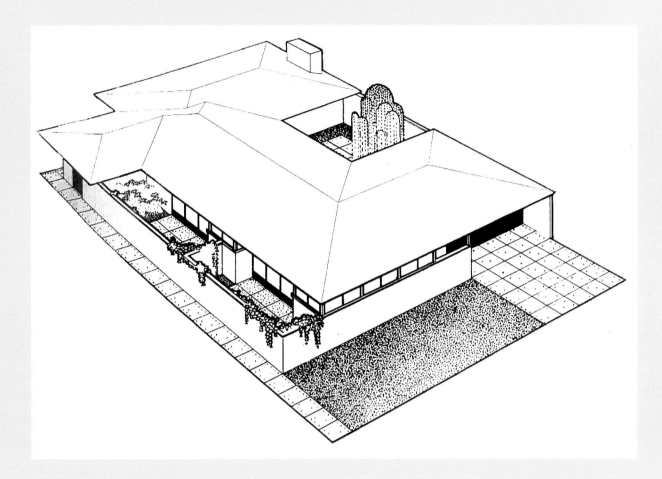

tecture), the board-and-batten walls (in place of the concrete bubble stone he originally considered) borrow from Louis Easton's Curtis Ranch, which Harris often passed on his way to the Lowe House site. The living room and dining room were one continuous space, setting Modern houses apart from the conventions at this time. The bedrooms formed a separate wing, each with its own patio.

As a modernist shaping the architecture to the client and site, Harris designed many kinds of homes, including cantilevered hillside homes like the 1940 Havens House in Berkeley. His career included explorations of the open plan in Japanese architecture, such as in the Fellowship Park House, the Streamline Moderne, the Craftsman aesthetic of the Greene brothers, and Wright's Hollyhock House. He did not use the overt Ranch imagery like May and Wurster (though he designed a Ranch for director John Huston in

Opposite and top: Lowe House, 1933, Altadena, California. Harwell Hamilton Harris, architect. Born in California's agricultural Riverside County and educated in Los Angeles, Harris grew up in a new suburban city of sprawling distance. Working for architect Richard Neutra, who had migrated from Vienna, Austria, to Los Angeles, Harris learned a Modernism as sophisticated as any in the world. He combined these two influences in the Lowe House, the first of many of his Ranch House designs, a suburban design with the low lines of the Prairie Style house and the board-and-batten walls of the nearby Craftsman style Curtis Ranch House by Louis Easton.

the San Fernando Valley that was never built).[35] His compact ground-hugging one-story residences—settled on suburban sites, linking inside with outside, and with broad hipped roofs—added significantly to the formal definition of the Contemporary Ranch House, and anticipated the form of the minimal Ranch houses to come after World War II. Allied with Wurster in the profession's eyes (they had been acquaintances since 1934), Harris was closely linked to the movement of West Coast Regional Modernism.

Frank Lloyd Wright, of course, never admitted any influence on his innate creativity. But when he re-emerged on the architectural scene in 1935 after two fallow decades, it was with two 'new' residential concepts: the high-end custom Fallingwater, and the average person's Usonian house, Wright's version of the one-story single family suburban home—in effect, Wright's Contemporary Ranch House.

The 1936 Jacobs House was the first Usonian in a series that would extend into the 1950s. Echoing Harris' solution for the suburban home, Wright turned nearly windowless brick walls to the street, while long walls of glass windows and doors opened onto the private backyard. The carport became an integral part of the facade of the house. Bedrooms were small and clustered in a wing.[36]

The Ranch House and Modern architecture were increasingly parallel trends. Both emphasized informal open plans to meet the needs of modern life and both expressed their structural elements. Yet the similarity was controversial. On the one hand, *Sunset magazine* attempted to claim everything that was not otherwise nailed down with a specific label as "Ranch" ("Today, almost any house that provides for an informal type of living and is not definitely marked by unmistakable style symbols is called a *ranch house.*")[37] As a styleless, purely functional expression of the house and the contemporary family lifestyle, *Sunset* considered the Ranch House as thoroughly Modern. On the other hand, academics and critics condemned Wurster and other Regionalist architects for incorporating historical and vernacular elements into their designs—accusing them of contaminating the pure expression of form and function.

Certainly the Ranch House as a popular style reflected new social patterns and lifestyles in the middle and upper-middle classes; over the decades, as servants became more expensive, homemakers took over the running of the house themselves, and architects and housing developers created plans that were easier, more convenient, and more conducive to raising families. The needs of children—such as play space inside and out—was another practical factor that reshaped the house. The result of these issues was an intersection of the Ranch House's moderate Modernism with traditional solutions and the demands of modern life and ideas.

Another point of congruence between the Ranch House and Modernism was the issue of indoor-outdoor design. But once again it was difficult to say that Modern architects had introduced the idea, as a blending of indoors and outdoors had been a part of the traditional working-ranch concept: where climate permitted, nineteenth-century porches and hacienda courtyards had made the outdoors a continuous part of the architecture and lifestyle of the residents. In the twentieth century, Modern architectural theory promoted the idea—especially in the work of avant-garde California architects like R. M. Schindler and Richard Neutra.

Likewise, Modernism's expression of structure was echoed in the Ranch's exposed-beam ceilings, post-and-beam structure, and exposed rafters along the eaves. The Ranch's rustic simplicity of construction and its direct, "honest" use of materials were repeated in Modernism's simple, unornamented aesthetic.

The Mature Ranch House

By 1940, the Ranch House was an accepted style for custom homes throughout the United States.[38] The original vernacular versions had been modified in form and plan as the Ranch House adapted to suburban lots and modern lifestyles.[39] Wurster's 1940 Reynolds House, outside Gilroy, initiated a series of his Ranch House designs, which, though derived from vernacular examples, lost the sense of a collection of vernacular sheds. Instead, the house was unified under long rambling gabled roofs. David Gebhard and Robert Winter use the Reynolds House as the definitive example of the California Ranch House in their *Guide to Northern California Architecture*.[40]

Architect Lutah Maria Riggs's 1939 Knemeyer House in Rolling Hills is a classic upper-middle class Ranch House of this period (see p. 86). It is suburban, but with a stable and a sizable lot for privacy; astounding views of the ocean lift the house into something close to an idealized vision of living in nature. The architecture is straightforward—using rustic board-and-batten siding, exposed rafters, and porches framed by rough-hewn wood posts—but without the heightened picturesqueness of Cliff May designs, or the visual austerity of Wurster. Wings are placed at irregular angles, taking advantage of the site to create a protected back patio. Elegant details and paneling recall the baronial aspect of the larger haciendas.

In New England, architect Royal Barry Wills's deft rendering of the Cape Cod style was also taking on aspects of the suburban Ranch House; the editors of *Architectural Forum* noted that Wills's 1939 house for Daniel H. Coakley Jr. in Buzzard's Bay Massachusetts, was "designed to give the effect of a 'rambling' house."[41] Almost as successful in promoting the Cape Cod through plan books and popular magazines as Cliff May was in promoting the Ranch House, Wills also had an appreciation of Modern ideas. He collaborated easily with his former employee, Hugh Stubbins Jr., on flat-roofed, starkly unornamented modern homes, even while he championed the Cape Cod home.[42]

In Texas, architect John Staub was contributing his own version of this mature Ranch House.[43] Based on a different model than the houses Williams and Ford admired and photographed in rural Texas—those were primarily small rural town homes—Staub's design borrowed from another wood vernacular tradition that could be found on working ranches in the Panhandle, west Texas, and indeed throughout the West. It was distinguished by a single long gabled structure,

Opposite: House, 1941, Massachusetts. Royal Barry Wills, architect. As Americans from the Pacific to the Atlantic moved to suburbia after World War II, the rambling, informally composed house known as the Ranch could be found across the nation. In New England, Royal Barry Wills popularized the form in houses and plan books. Instead of the board-and-batten walls of Western Ranch houses, he used Cape Cod Salt Box architectural elements: white clapboards, shuttered windows, steep roof slopes, and weather vanes. The popular Cape Cod style also influenced early mass-produced home designs, especially in the East, including the original Levittown house designs. The new single-family suburban postwar homes might have been given the popular Cape Cod label, but there were no "Easterns" playing during Saturday afternoon matinees at the Bijou. The growing media power of California and the West allowed the glamour of the highly popular Hollywood Western, redolent with adventure and independence, to rub off on the Ranch House as it helped to define an era, a lifestyle, and an architecture.

usually of log or wood, with a shallower roof pitch. The form was determined by the materials, the structure, and the climate; long, narrow houses, one-room deep, allowed natural cross-ventilation. The roof extended, usually at a slightly shallower slope, over porches on one or both sides, which were supported by wood posts.[44]

The large 1936 Ranch House Staub designed for Mr. and Mrs. Lamar Fleming Jr. on the Guadalupe River in Kerr County outside San Antonio, shows the influence of the West Texas ranch vernacular.[45] Most of the Texas limestone masonry house is one-room deep, to facilitate natural breezes. Porches face several rooms, with a door leading directly from each room to the outside. The house includes a breezeway between the living rooms and the bedrooms, reflecting the vernacular dogtrot house: two enclosed areas connected by a single roof with an open passage between to capture breezes and shade. Each succeeding wing is slightly set in and smaller, giving the impression of having been added on with time—reflecting the additive architecture that was typical of the vernacular working-ranch house. In the work of Cliff May, Royal Barry Wills, and John Staub, this practical characteristic of historic ranch houses becomes a sophisticated aesthetic form that tempers starkness by creating a means to introduce varied proportions to the building volumes.[46]

Though Ranch houses were built nationwide, due to a robust nineteenth-century ranching tradition and a large twentieth-century population, California played a major role in its development and dispersion. Texas was also a large state with a long and varied history, but it had a smaller population than California. Arizona and New Mexico shared a distinctive colonial and territorial culture as well as a ranching economy, but as states without large cities, their local culture did not evolve the same protean experimentation and breadth of architectural talent that California could boast from the 1880s on. In California these factors created the historic working-ranch precedents, produced the architects to draw from them in creative ways, generated the clients to commission the architects, and—in a historic confluence—sparked a population boom unlike any other after World War II. That boom would boost the Ranch House

as a hypercommodity that spread across the country—a quintessential story that reveals some of the basic forces shaping twentieth-century architecture and urbanism.

The Mass Produced Ranch House

The nineteenth-century working-ranch house was a plain-spoken industrial architecture—functional in organization, practical in materials, and stripped of frills. The twentieth-century Ranch House, in pointed contrast, transfigured that pragmatic, often crude architecture into a romantic image. The board-and-batten walls became not a simple structural system but a symbol of an appealing, self-sufficient past; exposed-plank ceilings were not simply functional but also quaint. But the story of the Ranch House held one more ironic twist: as it was repeated in literally hundreds of thousands of mass-produced tract homes, the Ranch House became, once again, an industrialized architecture—this time in its means of construction. Outstripping anything the Bauhaus produced, it applied the principle of twentieth-century assembly line manufacturing to housing for the masses.

For the first half of the twentieth century, the building industry in the United States was dominated by small builders and piecemeal development. Developers would buy property (often agricultural, on the edge of town) and legally subdivide the large sites into many small lots. They would often add streets and utilities. The lots would typically then be sold; individual families might buy a lot, hire an architect or builder, or send off for plans from a plan book or plan service. Homebuilders might buy several lots and build houses on speculation, or (with a real estate agent) find clients who wanted to build a house. The builder might use an architect, or buy plans from a selection offered by a plan service. Sometimes a well-funded developer would build an entire subdivision of houses at once; but neighborhoods tended to have a variety of house styles as they were filled in over the decades.

It was typical for ten or twenty houses to be built at a time. In 1939, "fewer than one-tenth of one percent of Los Angeles builders completed one hundred or more units," notes historian Greg Hise.[47] Building was also a strongly localized industry. Climate, unions, available materials, and

Left: Toluca Wood, 1941, San Fernando Valley, California. Marlow-Burns, developers. Though Wurster, May, Riggs, Harris, and other architects designed notable custom Ranch houses, developers such as Fred Marlow and Fritz Burns made the Ranch one of the most successful and widespread residential types in American architecture. Beginning in 1938 in Windsor Hills, by 1941 they had refined the mass-production techniques and the mass-marketed images that allowed the Ranch to be affordable to the broad middle class. This model is typical of the minimal Ranch designs they used in Westchester and elsewhere. Key to the success of these modest Ranch houses was the financing provided by FHA loans after 1934; FHA design standards also influenced the shape and features of these houses.

Right: Hillsdale development, 1940, San Mateo, California. David Bohannon, developer. Aspen Lane featured the initial model homes for Hillsdale, one of the few large planned communities begun before World War II. Simple gable roofs, front porches, asymmetric facades, and plain exposed wood rafter ends identify these homes as Ranch houses. (Compare it to the 1875 Harrell Ranch on p. 24.) Far from a replica of an actual house on a ranch, the Ranch House of twentieth-century suburbia is an original invention, one that mixes a dose of historical memory with a savvy response to the technology, demographics, and market forces of the middle twentieth century.

Opposite: Model house, c. 1948. David Bohannon, developer. Simple Ranch houses like this became a common sight in post-war America. The low-pitched roof, horizontal lines, and asymmetrical composition identify it as a Ranch House. Influenced by the abstracted, simplified lines of William Wurster, Gardner Dailey, and other Bay Area Regional Modernists (as well as mass-production techniques that encouraged simplification), Ranch houses often featured picturesque details such as board-and-batten walls, brick foundations, diamond-pane windows, and dovecotes.

public taste and demand all varied in a complex equation that could not be replicated exactly across the country; developers had to learn their territory. In treeless Phoenix, for example, concrete block was the preferred material; it stood up well to the heat, where wood would dry out. Before the end of the 1930s, however, several private builders across the country were themselves planning—and actually building—housing tracts on a scale never before attempted. The Ranch House was their favored type.

The laboratory of developer Marlow-Burns (Fred W. Marlow and Fritz B. Burns) was on the west side of Los Angeles: they built Windsor Hills (1938), a pleasant site on the southern slopes of Baldwin Hills overlooking the South Bay, not far from the earlier trendsetting Leimert Park development; in Westside Village (1939) at Overland and Venice Boulevards; in Westchester (1941) at Manchester and Sepulveda Boulevards; and in Toluca Wood (1941) in the San Fernando Valley.[48]

Marlow-Burns were community builders, not just housing developers; their approach was a strategic component for progressive developers. Parks, roads, schools, hospitals, and shopping centers (in Windsor Hills, designed by the prominent architect Stiles O. Clements) were planned as part of the communities they were building from scratch.[49] Key to these developments were the appeal and efficiency

of the house plan, the quality, safety, attractiveness, and diverse aspects of the community plan, and the cost efficiency and spread of construction methods.

At their first development at Windsor Hills, Marlow-Burns continued the conventional practice of subdividing and selling lots to individuals, builders, and speculators. But, for the first time, they also built a number of houses themselves. This was the first step to becoming full-fledged merchant builders, and they took the second step at Westside Village, organizing their operation for mass building and creating a staging area next to the building site for delivery of materials.[50] The design of the typical Marlow-Burns house was dictated to a large extent by the economics of building and the guidelines of the FHA (and later VA), which approved loans—an essential component to successful mass sales.[51] These guidelines dictated an efficient, square plan, which saved materials. Bedrooms were ganged to the side or to the rear; living room, dining area, and kitchen took up the other half of the house. Garages or carports may or may not have been included. The houses were one story and, in California, built on a concrete slab or on a perimeter foundation with floor joists with a crawl space beneath.

The plan mirrored the FHA guidelines for the minimum house, determined by scientific studies and developed in the guidelines, "Principles of Planning Small Houses."[52]

Top: Model house, c. 1950, San Francisco Bay Area. David Bohannon, developer. As the initial demand for postwar housing was met, developers began to offer more choices and larger homes (two-car garages, differing styles, etc.).

Middle: David Bohannon (left) poses in front of one of his model homes, a Contemporary Style Ranch House from the early 1950s. Developers such as Bohannon, in major cities across the country, built hundreds of thousands of Ranch houses between 1945 and 1970, making the type one of the most successful and widespread in American history.

Opposite: Bohannon House, 1938, Woodside Hills, California. Gardner Dailey, architect. Developer Bohannon commissioned Bay Area Modernist Gardner Dailey to design his own house in a new equestrian subdivision on the San Francisco peninsula. Though the large house had a flat roof, its sprawling wings and horizontal lines echoed those of Bohannon tracts. The house was featured at San Francisco's 1939 World's Fair.

Informal open floor plans were emerging in the 1930s (in the high-art designs of Harwell Hamilton Harris, Frank Lloyd Wright, and others), but the demands of the minimal house also encouraged blending rooms and functions—the dining room, in particular, combined with either the living room or the kitchen in many plans.[53] The efficient plan also owed much to the precedents of the Chicago bungalow and other inner-city worker homes on narrow lots.

Beyond those requirements that dictated the form and room arrangements, the design was determined by efficiencies of construction and market demand. The most obvious choice for a style, given the majority of designs in plan books, and the fashions for housing in the East, might have been Cape Cod: a steep-roofed, eaveless cottage with a central front door, balanced by two windows on either side. Instead, Marlow-Burns, David Bohannon, and other large-scale developers, built simplified Ranch Houses.[54] A sales photo of the "Defender" model by Marlow-Burns in Westchester underscores this connection between minimal affordable houses and the Ranch House. The name evokes both Fort Apache and the Arsenal of Democracy (many home buyers worked in nearby defense plants) in an artful blurring of the line between the Old West and modern suburbia—a line the Ranch House carefully straddled in advertising and design. It is a small house, but a front porch dominates the facade, and a carefully placed wagon wheel leans against a porch column, which is being admired by the homebuyers inspecting the house. Roof rafters are exposed, and a mudline (a change in paint color borrowed from the Spanish tradition) runs around the stuccoed house at the two-foot datum. With this model, the average homebuyer could have a ranch, a piece of the wide-open plains, and the lifestyle of a cowboy. The reasonable cost and the livable plan cemented the deal.

In addition to this Rancho-model type, ads for Marlow-Burn's 1941 Westchester development boasted the Suburban and the Cape Cod models. The distinctions were ornamental; the form of each was resolutely Ranch. The low ground-hugging profile, the asymmetry, the decorative elements focused on horizontality (even in perfectly square plans), the simple rooflines, the wide eaves rustically punctuated by exposed rafters—all of these were derived from the Ranch House as it had been developing for a decade and promoted in shelter magazines. The houses of Rolling Hills (not far from Westchester and Windsor Hills) were the obvious high-art relatives of this average person's house. Lutah Maria Riggs's 1939 Knemeyer House shows each of these elements, though on a larger and more elaborate scale (see p. 86). The Ranch House was becoming a democratic architecture, appealing to working and upper classes alike. During and after World War II, tens of thousands of minimal Ranch Houses like those of Marlow-Burns in Westchester were built. It ranked with the Craftsman-style bungalow, the Chicago bungalow, and the Victorian rowhouse as one of the most popular choices for American living.

In 1940, a similar Ranch House development emerged in the Hillsdale subdivision on the San Francisco peninsula, by builder David Bohannon. Hillsdale, like Marlow-Burns's Westchester development, was conceived on a remarkably large scale. To achieve sales, the entire organization of construction had to be rethought. A major element of this process was the cutting yard, a staging and preparation lot where the individual studs, lintels, plates, and rafters were cut *en masse* for smooth and speedy delivery to the building sites nearby. Once construction ended, the cutting yard site became a commercial setting for the community. *Architectural Forum,* in June 1945, reported that Bohannon first introduced pre-cutting of lumber for this project. Bohannon's construction superintendent had experience in large-scale building projects; he had worked on both the Boulder Dam and the Golden Gate Bridge.

Bohannon built sixteen "exhibit homes" for his "huge Hillsdale tract," designed by the architecture firm of Williams and Wastell. Ophelia Kroger Bohannon, David's wife, helped refine the house plans; she insisted, for instance, on a front hall to help the circulation pattern in the houses.[55] The two- and three-bedroom model homes on Arbor Lane West, selling for $5,000–$6,000, were identified as "California Ranch houses" in sales brochures, though other similar models were labeled Cape Cod (distinguished by a quaint bay window, or Colonial light fixtures over the door). Long and low, functionally and aesthetically asymmetrical in composition, with an

ornamental rustic bracket or dovecote over the garage, these houses were essentially Ranch.

Unlike the Marlow-Burns square-plan houses, these Hillsdale houses were rectangular. The long gabled roof stretched along the lot, emphasizing the long, low rambling profile. A porch with the front door was set into the volume, framed by wood columns. The roof was shingled; wide eaves were trimmed plainly with exposed rafter ends—an unfinished rustic look that gave the home a desirably informal flavor. The walls were board or stucco, and the windows were flanked by shutters. Glass windows and doors lead to the backyard—a clear statement of the Ranch lifestyle.

The advertising billboard at Highway 101 and 31st Avenue read, "Live and Play in Hillsdale—an Achievement in Community Planning." Around this time, planners and academics, including Catherine Bauer Wurster and Lewis Mumford, as well as certain developers, including Bohannon and Burns, believed firmly in the need to create a community rooted in the Garden City concepts of Ebenezer Howard—with parks, schools, and shopping centers, laid out in a pleasing and safety-conscious plan of streets.[56] To the public, such planning implied a higher level of quality—a chief selling point. At Hillsdale, with its own new Bohannon-built railroad station, commuters could conveniently ride to jobs in San Francisco or San Jose, which was a key element in good planning.[57]

Central to this concern for planning was the street. The conscious arrangement and relationship of houses created a varied prospect which was appealing to potential home buyers. On this academic level planners and developers agreed: "Most important in creating an attractive development of standard small homes is land planning and subdivision pattern," wrote David Bohannon in 1940. "The project must be planned as a whole, and a house placed on each lot so as to have good orientation and elevation detail giving the feeling of variety with the range of vision. At least sixteen distinctive elevations should be used—twenty or twenty-four can be created from one floor plan. Color and exterior materials deserve expert handling. . . . To avoid monotony . . . there must be a number of roof elevations. Landscape will do the rest."[58] This balance of individuality and variety was to become a major theme in Ranch House subdivisions; it was a notable conceptual shift from earlier housing tracts, such as for the Chicago bungalow, where the neat repetition of similar forms sharply delineated by the narrow lots that sited houses cheek by jowl, was considered aesthetically desirable. As Bohannon pitched, "One of the basic ideas on which Hillsdale is founded is architectural harmony among all homes . . . safeguarding the investment of those who buy in Hillsdale."[59]

Nearby shopping was another critical factor in community building. J. C. Nichols, the father of the modern shopping center, visited Bohannon and advised him to include a shopping district in the development. In 1941, Bohannon had attracted Sears to the shopping center on El Camino Real adjacent to the Hillsdale tract; as the area grew he expanded with Hillsdale Shopping Center (Welton Becket Associates, architects) in late 1953, breaking ground with the inclusion of Macy's first suburban store on the West Coast—a bellwether of the direction of cities and planning.[60]

Even before World War II, the Ranch homes of Hillsdale, Westchester, and Toluca Wood had become modern artifacts built by modern machines and planned by the techniques of modern manufacturing, for the modern consumer. But their

David Dewey Bohannon

Bohannon (1898–1995) had been a real estate salesman and a small-scale home developer since 1932, when he sold the Belle Haven City subdivision near Palo Alto. On this tract of twenty homes, he offered lots, plans, and specs for the usual mix of Spanish, Tudor, and fairy tale cottage-style homes found in many California tracts of the 1920s and early 1930s.[61] He then bought up land tracts from old estates on the San Francisco Peninsula and built his first tract, Embarcadero Oaks in Palo Alto in 1936, under the name of Suburban Builders, Inc., hiring Wallace A. Stephen as the supervising architect for his organization. The houses were American Colonial Revival, Monterey Revival, and Tudor Revival cottage in style. At Oak Knoll, a related development on Foothill Boulevard at 82nd Avenue in Oakland, Bohannon built twenty homes in the first phase in 1936, with a total of 300 planned.

Styles in the tract ranged from Colonial to Ranch—already a popular and acceptable style for West Coast middle-class homes. Though these homes were built on two levels fitted into the hillside site (with the one-car garage tucked underneath), the clean modern lines of board siding and exposed rustic rafter ends identified them as Ranches.[62]

As an expert salesman, Bohannon used advertising and publicity to help sell his homes, publicizing his tracts in local papers and national magazines like *McCalls*. His own 1938 house, designed by Gardner Dailey in Woodside Hills, was chosen as a *Good Housekeeping* Magazine Model House for the 1939 San Francisco World's Fair at Treasure Island; along with the other new houses around the Bay Area (including two William Wurster homes), it was open for tours during the run of the Fair.[63] Displays and brochures showed off the flat-roofed modern one-story house

with wide eaves. Like Cliff May's houses of the period, the plan displayed the same angled-bedroom wing that created a courtyard. The design, said a brochure, "was not in conformity with any style—but was an interpretation of a mode of living."[64] With furnishings from the City of Paris department store, a pool, and landscaping by Thomas Church, the $45,000 house was comfortably upper-middle class in a new subdivision of custom homes. Suburban Builders Inc. built several houses (designed by architects Chester H. Triechel and Albert H. Larson) in the upscale neighborhood. These were Ranch style too, with porches, gabled roofs, and rambling wings considered suitable for the rolling grassy hills of northern California. The upper-class imagery (an English rider with a bob-tail horse graced the tract's logo) was echoed in the Colonial ornamentation of these rambling Ranches.[65]

With such momentum, Bohannon, in 1940, planned his next step: a 400-home community (five thousand homes projected) called Hillsdale in San Mateo, halfway between San Francisco and San Jose on the San Francisco peninsula.

Belle Haven model house, 1932, Palo Alto, California. David Bohannon, developer. This Spanish-style house was typical of the historical revival styles popular in the 1920s and 1930s among custom and tract homebuyers. The porch with French doors (set in a Moorish arch) shows the ongoing interest in indoor-outdoor spaces in California architecture.

domestication of Modernism also reflected the public's equal acceptance of historic imagery and cultural meaning. They did not require architecture to be, in the insistence of Modern theory, brutally "honest." They did not require buildings to look like machines simply because they were built with the aid of machines.

War Housing and the Ranch House

World War II catapulted the housing industry into the future, just as it did to the electronics and aerospace industries. Government commissions, loans, and allocations of materials encouraged large-scale housing for workers attracted to locales where there were critical defense jobs. California gained more than its share. Shipworkers flocked to the shipyards in Sausalito, Richmond, and Vallejo; aircraft workers moved to Santa Monica, Torrance, the San Fernando Valley, Long Beach, and San Diego. This largesse of jobs gave high-art Modern architects, including William Wurster, Richard Neutra, and Hugh Stubbins, Jr., opportunities to build on a larger scale than ever before, and to apply and refine building systems based on modules and prefabrication—an ongoing obsession, it seemed, of the architectural profession.[66] But significant lessons and experiences were also learned by developers such as David Bohannon, and Abraham, William, and Alfred Levitt, who built with the aid of Title VI allocations that funneled materials and labor to defense-related housing.[67] They honed their mass building skills in defense housing—and then directly applied those valuable lessons to numerous Ranch houses in the decades after the war.[68] "The building of 500 to more than 1,300 homes at a time in a single project under the pressure of wartime urgency, has given us an opportunity to develop production techniques that would normally not be used in a moderate building program," reported *American Builder* in 1943.[69]

The war halted Bohannon's incomplete Hillsdale development, but unlike many housing developers, who, daunted by wartime restrictions on materials and labor, dropped out for the duration, Bohannon used the war to continue the exploration of mass-production techniques he had begun at Hillsdale: some 212 units of housing in Sunnyvale near a submarine facility, 700 units at Rollingwood in Richmond

near the Kaiser Shipyard, and 559 units at Westwood Napa, near the Vallejo shipyards. In these and similar projects Bohannon honed the methods and skills that permitted the creation of the enormous Ranch House tracts of the 1950s. Bohannon's 700 houses built in 700 working hours (693 to be exact) at Rollingwood was thus praised in 1942: "A combination of precutting and line assembly systems were selected as the most efficient and fastest method," wrote a contemporary magazine. It was the same concept used at Hillsdale, but the added pressure to house defense workers quickly refined the system under the direction of Bohannon's partner H. A. Chamberlain, a private builder of homes before the war. Lumber purchase orders created a cutting list for each of the two basic house models. Individual pieces of lumber for 200 houses were stockpiled before groundbreaking began to assure the smooth flow of materials. The flow of materials and tradespeople had to be organized so that delivery to each house site occurred at the right time, keeping up a continual and efficient flow of construction; one late delivery could throw the process behind.

Electric hand saws kept the process moving rapidly. Individual crews specialized in each step of the process: building foundation forms, pouring concrete, stripping forms, placing mud sills, girders and joists, laying subfloor, erecting stud walls and ceiling joists, framing the roofs, sheathing, and plastering. The lack of skilled labor due to

the war actually encouraged breaking down the building process into simple actions that could be taught to unskilled laborers—as the assembly line had done for the automobile industry thirty years earlier. "Materials and operations moved forward on the site instead of products moving forward over the machinery," reported a trade journal. The factory was taken to the field.[70]

This method also shaped and streamlined the architecture itself, eliminating details or shapes in the plan that wasted time or materials. The one-story houses were simple, with two or three bedrooms; the latter also offered an attached one-car garage. The plan mirrored FHA standards, dividing space between the public living room (with dining nook) and separate kitchen on one half, and the private bedrooms on the other. One bedroom with an exterior door was designated as a rental for a non-family war worker. Shops were included in the community plan at the main entry to the development.

Rollingwood homes were minimal Ranch houses, comparable to the Marlow-Burns houses at Westchester, and those that would be seen in the great plats of Panorama City and Lakewood after the war. They were one story, with a small porch at the front door, and horizontal tongue-and-groove siding facing the street facade. The gable end was finished in vertical boards, whose lower ends were trimmed in a decorative scallop. By mixing L-shaped plans with garages

Left: Mortsolf House, 1947, Atherton, California. William Wurster, architect. The L-shaped plan, wide eaves, porches, wood siding, and casual composition of the Mortsolf House virtually define the Ranch House style. Rendered in Wurster's elegant proportions and understated details, the Ranch House is seen as the artistic equal of other Modern residential types.

Right: Model house, San Lorenzo Village, 1944, San Lorenzo, California. David Bohannon, developer. Wartime housing by Bohannon at Vallejo, Richmond, San Lorenzo, and other military defense plant sites created a template for the mass-produced housing to come in the boom years of the 1950s. The two- or three-bedroom homes were small; their wood-frame structure was easily reduced to simple steps that teams of unskilled workers could follow.

Zimmerman House, 1951, Manchester, New Hampshire. Frank Lloyd Wright, architect. Wright's Prairie house designs introduced the open interior plan and the horizontal profile to sub-urban American architecture a half century before the Zimmerman House was built. His flat-roofed Usonian house designs, beginning with the Herbert Jacobs House in 1936, also offered an affordable $5,000 house for the average family. Though Wright did not identify such designs as this as Ranch houses, their gabled roofs, horizontal lines, open plans, and integration of indoors and outdoor repeated the themes already developed in the Ranch. Wright's prominence, however, influenced numerous architects designing Contemporary Style Ranch houses without traditional Ranch ornament.

and square plans without garages, the master plan mini-mized the repetitive character of mass-produced housing along the curving streetscapes. An image of individuality was still critical to consumer acceptance of mass-produced housing—a concern no one seemed to have for mass pro-duced Flying Fortresses or Liberty Ships.

In 1944, Bohannon's San Lorenzo Village took Rollingwood a step further with a more sophisticated master plan. It was a model city of 1,500 homes for defense workers and for workers of planned Chrysler and National Automotive Fibre Company plants, both of which had purchased property nearby.[71] The shopping district built on the fabrication yard used during construction included a supermarket (James M. Mitchell, architect), a restaurant (Douglas Dacre Stone and Lou B. Mulloy, architects), and a handsome Late Moderne theater (Alex A. Carter, architect).[72]

The construction techniques refined those at Rollingwood and the lessons of wartime construction were directly applied: foundation "ditching at San Lorenzo rivaled Seabee

speed," reported *Architectural Forum*. The master plan fea-tured small loop roads off of the two main east/west thorough-fares in order to keep through-traffic out of neighborhoods. The house plans were more generous than Rollingwood's, though only slightly larger. The three-bedroom homes (initially without garages) featured a stub wing for the living room and included a fireplace, while the kitchen on the back corner had light on two sides and its own entrance.

High-art architects, in their quest to bring good design to the mass audience, also built defense housing and experimented with mass-construction methods. Most designs were attached housing in two-story blocks, but single-family homes were also built.[73]

Richard Neutra's 1942 Progressive Builders' Homes in Burbank were one of a series of low-cost housing projects he designed in the 1930s and 1940s. Sponsored by the FHA and located near the Lockheed Aircraft factory, Neutra's version of the small house bore similarities to the homes that Fritz Burns was building in Westchester around the

Before the Boom

same time. Notable were the simple gabled roofs with wide eaves (rare in Neutra's career) anchored by a brick chimney. Unlike Burns's houses, Neutra's made no nod to historic detailing. A porch faced the small backyard; each house in the block of detached homes had a living room extending from front to back, and bedrooms along the front of the house. Only fourteen of these homes were built.[74]

For the war effort, William Wurster designed one- and two-story attached apartment units (at Carquinez Straits) and single-family homes (Parker Homes, Sacramento, 1943).[75] He obtained federal funding to experiment with different structures conducive to mass production, including frame bents, wood skeleton frames, and masonry units. As at Rollingwood, the plain character of these low-cost designs dictated simplicity, which Wurster interpreted in open plans; in Carquinez, for example, kitchens were separated from the living area by only a curtain.

Despite the ingenuity and sophistication of these high-art proposals for mass housing, none had an impact on post-war suburban tract house development. Many developers distrusted architects—especially those with well known reputations—and many architects in turn were (with significant exceptions) not willing to adjust their designs to the constraints of the practical marketplace.

Merchant builders were to write most of the next chapter in the history of the Ranch House. High-art architects had been beguiled by the simple lines of vernacular adobe, stone, and wood working-ranch homes; however, the real impact of the Ranch House would emerge as it began to satisfy the aspirations of a newly prosperous, newly enlarged middle class. Workers who had lived in crowded cities could now live in open, spacious suburbs. The Ranch House hinted at the openness, the personal freedom, and the rugged individuality of the Western myth, which had long since vanished; and, yet, a backyard of one's own offered a piece of that myth to more and more Americans as they moved freely to the new suburbs.

Left: Markham House, 1940, Palm Springs, California. Albert Frey, architect. Though known for his adventurous Modern designs, Swiss emigré Frey built or remodeled almost forty of the eighty Ranch homes in Palm Springs' Smoke Tree Ranch. The community's strict design guidelines dictated the Ranch style (one-story homes, shake roofs of a specific slope, attached garages), but Frey's Ranch designs show the same originality as his Modern designs and are a serious aspect of his work.

Right: House, c. 1948, Kingman Avenue, Santa Monica, California. The minimal Ranch, like this example, was a simplified version of the Ranch House. Its asymmetrical facade, hipped or gabled roof, and wide eaves could be seen in large tract examples such as Kaiser Homes' Panorama City in the San Fernando Valley. Often only a simple ornamental gesture or roofline was needed to convey the image of Ranch in a design.

Popular Mechanics Ranch House, 1951, Portland, Oregon. John J. Whalen, architect. Writer Tom Riley built this house for $7,450 with his wife Vinita and a few friends, and wrote about the experience in the pages of *Popular Mechanics* magazine. As one measure of the immense popularity of the Ranch House, its plans were offered in the popular magazine to any reader so that they could build their own Ranch House.

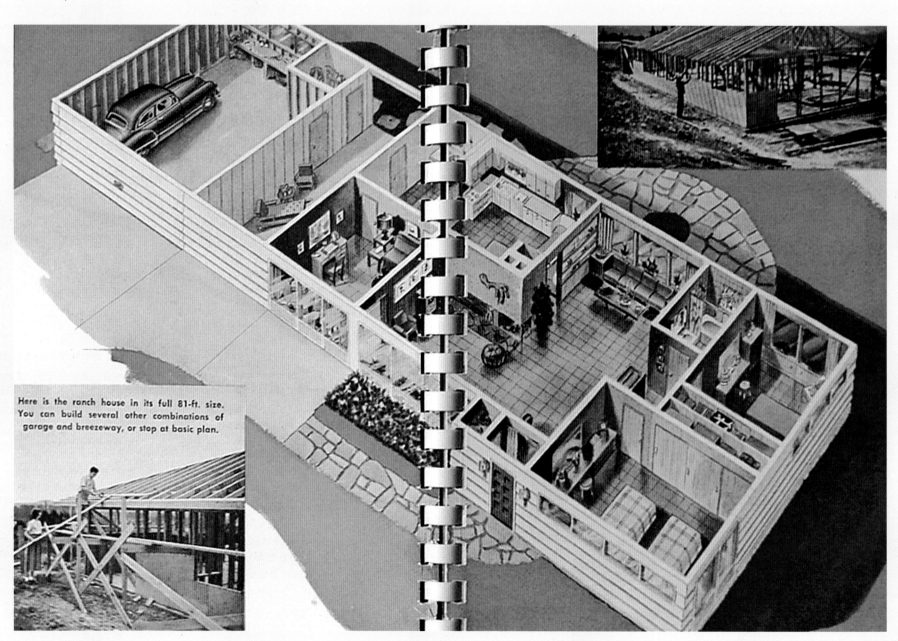

Here is the ranch house in its full 81-ft. size. You can build several other combinations of garage and breezeway, or stop at basic plan.

The Ranch House at the Peak:

After the War

"A California-styled house—like the ranch type—built in a carefully planned neighborhood or community with all the essentials for good living is your best bet for the post-war," said a housing industry report in 1945, evidence that the Ranch was already not only well established before the war, but a favored style for the future.[1]

With the war over, a generation that had been living in substandard, crowded housing in inner cities was demanding housing of its own, with yards and plenty of space to raise families. The challenges to the building industry were daunting. How was it to organize the building of five hundred or one thousand homes—or more—at a time? Where were the materials and skilled labor to come from? How was the process to be organized efficiently? Could costs be kept down so houses would be affordable to the mass market? Would the banking industry be able to process a flood of mortgage applications, let alone have the resources to fund them? And above all, what did the public want in a house? Clearly, four walls and a roof were not enough. The ending of the war launched a decade of housing experimentation as builders and architects sought the formula to an appealing and efficient mass-built house. In addition, museums and newspapers sponsored exhibits and books on the postwar house. Copper and appliance manufacturers did the same, in order to promote the use of their products. Department stores built full-scale home models, complete with their brand lines of furnishings, and Ranch Houses were displayed at home shows.[2] The FHA established guidelines for construction and plans. Publishing houses printed magazines and books of house plans and guidance for the postwar homebuyer. And, of course, architecture magazines weighed in on the issue regularly; Time Incorporated created an entire magazine, House + Home, which focused exclusively on the subject.

The mainstream enthusiasm for the Ranch inspired the magazine Popular Mechanics to publish a book on the "Popular Mechanics Build-it-Yourself Ranch-Type House" in 1951. The magazine claimed, "This 'dream house' was born of the many requests of the readers of Popular Mechanics magazine for the plans of a modern ranch-type house." Designed by architect John J. Whalen, it was built for $7,450 in Portland, Oregon, by author Tom Riley with the help of his wife Vinita and a few friends.[3]

Housing developers stood at the forefront of the Ranch effort. The large housing developers of the postwar period came from a variety of backgrounds. San Francisco's David Bohannon was the consummate realtor, "a strapping, six-foot master salesman," according to Colliers magazine, which tagged him "the Henry J. Kaiser of the housing industry"—a bit presumptuous, considering Henry J. Kaiser himself was also active in the postwar housing industry. Kaiser was partnered with Los Angeles's Fritz Burns, another real-estate man who already had experience in drawing together pieces of the puzzle to increase the scale of housing.[4] Northern California's Joseph Eichler was an egg and butter man, early retired, who became fascinated with a new industry and a new aesthetic. Phoenix's John F. Long was a tinkerer in the tradition of Henry Ford, constantly observing and experimenting, improving and streamlining systems to reduce costs and maximize profits. Philip Klutznick of American Community Builders in Chicago was a government-housing bureaucrat who mastered the critical minutiae of finance and organizational detail. In short, most major cities had large housing developers, though telling their individual stories is beyond the scope of this book. Highlighting a few representatives, however, will help illuminate the Ranch's transformation and dispersion as a national style.[5]

Sherman Park model "A" home, 1952, Reseda, California. Edward Fickett, architect; Ray Hommes Co., builder. After initial resistance by some developers, the Contemporary Style Ranch House soon became a favorite of many. USC-trained architect Ed Fickett initially designed Traditional Ranches, but gradually convinced his clients that Modern imagery, spaces, and post-and-beam construction could also sell well. The staggered-panel wall hanging from the wood posts screens the carport. This two-bedroom model first sold for $10,200.

Opposite: Cliff May Homes, model, 1953, West Covina, California. Cliff May, designer; Chris Choate, architect. The design used a post-and-beam structure, board-and-batten siding, and emphasized access to outdoor terraces, just as did May's larger custom homes; the same structure and indoor-outdoor plan was also seen in high-art Modern designs for the Case Study program and the Modernist Eichler Home subdivisions.

Two Visions for Postwar Homes: The Case Study Program and Kaiser Community Homes

It was clear to many that the key to affordable housing lay in the application of mass-production assembly methods. There was less agreement, however, on how to apply those lessons learned in Detroit plants and wartime shipyards.[6] In the hopeful glow of Allied victory, both architects and developers proposed several visionary or futuristic schemes.

The leading architects of the day regularly offered proposals for mass housing using inventive modular systems, standardized steel structures, and prefabrication; none of these were applied by the large merchant builders.[7] Probably the best-known high-art proposal for postwar housing was the Case Study Program, started in 1946 and sponsored by editor John Entenza's *Arts + Architecture* magazine, which published many of the most innovative young architects of the day. By designating certain developing projects that fit the parameters of a "Case Study House," Entenza assured publicity, and a donation of materials and equipment for the house. In theory, the program aimed directly at the application of new construction systems in well-designed open plans to aid in the postwar housing crisis; in reality, however, it catered to the custom rather than the mass homebuyer.

Though Case Study steel-frame houses seemed to promise a rapid, logical building system that would revolutionize the industry, the real impact on cutting costs lay in simpler technologies: the process that reduced carpentry to an assembly line of discrete actions also reduced the need for costly skilled carpentry labor.[8] Yet, the program gained widespread popularity for its forward-looking buildings; Case Study homes featured in the *Los Angeles Times Home Magazine* attracted crowds to open houses. In contrast to the gabled roofs and board walls of the Ranch House, the Case Study's crisp steel frame (or wood post-and-beam structures) permitted enormous walls of glass and flat roofs—the epitome of the Modern City of Tomorrow. However, in terms of the actual number of houses built, the Case Study Program had a negligible effect on the housing market in Los Angeles and other cities. Among the Case Study architects, only A. Quincy Jones and Fred Emmons made any significant contribution to mass housing in the postwar period with their designs for the Eichler homes.[9]

It is still intriguing to note, however, how many of the Case Study architects also designed easily and skillfully in the Ranch House style. The line between straightforward Modern houses and the Ranch House was not always easy to define. Sumner Spaulding, architect of several Rolling Hills Ranch houses, designed Case Study House #2 in 1945–47 with John Rex. William Wurster also designed Case Study houses, as did J. R. Davidson, who designed the first Case Study house that was built.[10] Entenza invited Harwell Hamilton Harris (architect of the editor's own home in Brentwood) to design a Case Study house, but Harris refused for personal reasons. The fact that so many Modern designers contributed to the Ranch's evolution indicates how modern the Ranch House was.[11] In its tract-house version, the Ranch House employed modern prefabrication to speed production and lower costs.

Other visionary schemes to solve the housing crisis focused on the solution seemingly promised by the astonishing output of wartime shipyards and airplane factories.[12] "One of the most-talked about and least-understood products of twentieth-century technology—along with the atomic bomb—is the prefabricated house," wrote the authors of a

1947 book on prefab housing.[13] "To the uninitiated the word 'prefabrication' conjures up visions of houses rolling off assembly lines like so many automobiles, all neatly packaged and delivered ready for setting upon a chosen site." The book included seven pages of prefabricated home manufacturers across the nation in its appendix. Everyone from well-known architects to *Popular Mechanics* magazine shared the opinion of Kaiser housing division executive Howard Lindbergh in 1944: "There is no question in my mind that someday the gap will be bridged . . . to the mass production of complete houses in central factories."[14]

If anyone could make the factory-produced prefabricated house a reality, it was Henry J. Kaiser (1882–1967), one of the most famous industrialists of the era. Kaiser's philosophy of social progressivism (usually in conjunction with a masterful use of Federal funding) made him a controversial figure, yet his accomplishments could not be denied. He had launched his national building career as president of the Six Companies consortium that built the legendary Hoover Dam in the early 1930s. During the war, Kaiser Shipyards attained a fabled status as they churned out ships at an astounding rate; America's ability to out-produce the Germans and the Japanese proved a pivotal factor in the Allied victory. After the war the expanding Kaiser empire produced steel, aluminum, cement, home appliances, automobiles—and, of course, houses.[15] Developer Fritz Burns joined forces with Henry J. Kaiser to head his Kaiser Community Homes division. Howard Lindbergh initiated planning for a factory-assembly building for Kaisercraft Homes in Richmond, California, on the site of the former Kaiser Shipyard.[16] In 1946 Kaiser Community Homes actually built a plant on Manchester Boulevard to fabricate walls and other elements to be shipped to their building sites all over the Southland.[17]

Yet by 1949 it was clear to many that the dreams of prefabrication spurred by the spectacularly successful war factories were not going to bring a revolution in housing. "So far this method of building has not proved the panacea for all our housing ills, though perhaps in the future such methods of sectional off-the-site building will help reduce prices drastically and produce the ideal budget house,"

wrote William J. Hennessey, architectural and building research editor for *The American Home* magazine.[18]

With time and experience it became clear that the factory had to be taken to the field, the machine to the garden. The assembly-line methods, the efficient organization and flow of materials, the skilled and unskilled labor had to be arrayed on site, supplemented by some off-site prefabrication.

This system would take the Ranch House to the mass public. This is the direction Fritz Burns began before the war, and which he continued with Kaiser Community Homes in Panorama City in 1948—bringing affordable, decent housing to working-class homebuyers. Immediately after the war, Fritz Burns hired the dynamic, young Los Angeles architecture firm of Walter Wurdeman and Welton Becket to design the 1946 Postwar House, a model house in the heart of the Wilshire district to whet the public's appetite for new housing ideas. "We are building this house in order to make everybody in America dissatisfied with the homes they are living in now," boasted the head of publicity for Kaiser Community Homes.[19] Published in *House Beautiful* in May 1946, it incorporated every new appliance, material, and—most significantly—a modern open plan. With luxurious flagstone accent walls and an extensive outdoor patio and barbecue, it was far more lavish than any prewar Marlow-Burns house. Rather, with its low lines it was closer in style to a Contemporary Ranch House.

Wurdeman and Becket also designed model homes for Panorama City. Advertised as "Kaiser's 'California Ranch House'," the homes followed the basic minimal Ranch House plan seen before the war at Westchester and San Lorenzo Village, though on a larger scale and supplemented by more planned shopping areas, parks, and schools.[20] The lines were clear and simple with overhanging eaves and a mix of roof shapes for visual variety. In 1949, there were 1,529 single-family homes built; the two-bedroom 800-square-foot model sold for $9,000-$10,000; a three-bedroom home sold for $10,000 or more.

Repeating Burns's commitment to community building, the 60,000-square-foot Panorama City Shopping center opened in May 1952, and a Broadway department store followed in 1956. Movie theaters and bowling alleys were

The Ranch House at the Peak: The Tract

added. Showing the growing economic and demographic clout of suburbs, retail sales in the San Fernando Valley in 1955 surpassed those in the traditional shopping area of downtown Los Angeles.[21] The nearby site of a new General Motors plant (designed by Parkinson and Parkinson with Albert Kahn Associates) made the old Panorama Ranch property an ideal location for new housing on this scale.

Kaiser Community Homes also built San Fernando Valley homes on 400 acres south of Roscoe, and Woodman Avenue homes in 1950. Other Kaiser communities were built in San Jose, California, and Portland, Oregon, near Kaiser manufacturing facilities. The leap in numbers of units and the complexity of construction is astonishing. The seminal Leimert Park development had been 230 acres with 1,200 lots in 1929; Panorama City was 800 acres with 3,000 housing units in 1948. Though Walter Leimert had exploited economies of scale in Leimert Park, he had left most of the building, financing, and commercial development to others. At Panorama City a single company had done it all.

The Spread of the Tract Ranch House

Planned communities were being built in many cities in the years following the War, many of which applied the Ranch House style. The best known of these is Levittown—which began in 1949 on Hempstead, Long Island, New York—where a four-room Cape Cod-style house sold for $7,990. With 5,000 homes built initially there and later more in Pennsylvania, it was an enormous tract, but by no means the only one or the earliest example of mass-produced housing. Houston's Frank Sharp built 4,000 Ranch houses in Oak Forest in 1946, and Sharpstown, in southwest Houston, contained 25,000 homes plus shopping, offices, and recreational facilities on 6,500 acres begun in 1954; a three-bedroom brick Ranch House sold for $14,500. South of Chicago, American Community Builders began erecting Park Forest's 5,500 single-family homes in 1952; the first were inspired by Levitt's Cape Cod cottage, while later models borrowed from the Ranch style. And, beginning in 1954, John F. Long planned 25,000 homes at Maryvale in Phoenix. With these enormous tracts, the small Ranch House evolved as a new prototype for the

average American home for the population tide moving to the suburbs: it was one story, asymmetrical, with simple plans and a backyard.[22]

The tract housing of Lakewood, California, also gained national attention. The first of 17,500 houses was put up for sale in March 1950, and the last just three years later. Three businessmen, Mark Taper, Louis Boyar, and Ben Weingart, bought most of the property in 1949 because of its proximity to the Douglas Aircraft assembly and North American Aviation plants built in 1940.[23] Lakewood's publicity was prompted by the astonishment and skepticism of Eastern magazines. The aerial photographs published in these magazines of houses under construction on a barren, dusty

Maryvale, 1955, Phoenix, Arizona. John F. Long, developer. The premieres of supermarkets, fall car previews, and subdivisions inspired spectacular suburban civic events like this one for Maryvale. National press covered its opening week, which attracted 24,000 visitors. The 2,000-acre development eventually housed 100,000 people. Some Ranch House neighborhoods, now historical, are today being rediscovered for their mid-century exoticism. Others play a different but even more vital role in the urban economy: far from gentrified, Phoenix's Maryvale today provides inexpensive entry-level housing for yet another generation of homeowners.

Tract home, c. 1955, Phoenix, Arizona. John F. Long, developer. Floor-to-ceiling picture windows and simple planes of glass and stucco reflect the Contemporary Style Ranch aesthetic of this tract house. The free-form pool and covered patio responded to the desert climate. The sheer size of the California housing market made its trends influential nationally as developers borrowed the West Coast's lifestyle ideas and merchandising cachet.

square feet, the houses followed the FHA guidelines, which, in combination with the restraints of volume production to reduce materials and costs, resulted in a simple, square plan with a compact arrangement of living areas and bedrooms.[25]

Lakewood began with seven models—Paul Duncan was identified in brochures as the architect—but over time the models were revised and improved. As in all tract developments, a major design consideration was achieving a sense of individuality in houses that were as mass produced as Tupperware containers. Each model offered varied exteriors; gable ends faced the street on some, a hipped roof on others. Horizontal or vertical board-and-batten siding, or front or side entry doors altered the appearance of the facades. The models were mixed to create a random streetscape, with no two identical models next door or across the street from each other; the development's planners were well aware of the negative image of cookie-cutter houses. The master plan laid out a large rectangular grid (rather than the curving and diagonal streets of Panorama City); certain streets were designated parkways, with secondary streets parallel to them to cut down on the speed of traffic and increase the safety and quiet of the neighborhoods. Buffer streets paralleled the major arterials as a set back for the houses lining them.

A Third Postwar Vision:
The *Sunset* Book of Ranches with Cliff May

House Beautiful, Better Homes and Gardens, American Home, Sunset, and a score of popular general-audience magazines aimed at homeowners and homemakers played a critical role in spreading the look and the idea of the Ranch House in the postwar period.

Sunset, as the reigning Western lifestyle magazine, adopted a mission of establishing the Ranch in the public conscience. In 1946, the magazine published a book, *Sunset Western Ranch Houses,* in collaboration with designer Cliff May that gave potential homebuyers a wish list to pore over, a vision to aspire to, and ideas to apply. The book also proposed a philosophy of living centered around informality, outdoor living, gracious entertaining, natural materials, and

plain remained for some observers a powerful image of robotic mass production and suburban alienation. However, Lakewood quickly developed both landscaping (eucalyptus trees were planted along the streets) and a sense of community and family life, as described by D. J. Waldie in *Holy Land,* his memoir of growing up in Lakewood. The houses were small, and often siblings shared rooms. There were backyards, but the front yards and streets were utilized by kids playing ball—a very different, more human image than was implied by the spectacular, mechanistic aerial views published and republished.[24]

Lakewood houses followed the prewar design, bearing strong similarities to Ranch House developments such as a reliance on do-it-yourself. Even in the refined pages of *House Beautiful* in April 1946, May boasted about the casual lifestyle of the Ranch House: "We eat all over the house. . . . We don't like pretentious architecture."[26] His wife Jean spoke of spilling milk in the house without concern.

In their two books with *Sunset*, May and the editors carefully painted the Ranch House owner of the mid-twentieth century into the panorama of Western life since the 1840s. It was not a matter of following tradition; it was a way of life that, according to May, was unique and fitting to the benign climate, the adventurous culture, and the rich Western landscape to be explored and enjoyed. Standing firmly on the Ramona myth of Helen Hunt Jackson, May credited the Spanish with contributing a way of living "in a new and gentle place" isolated from the harsh worlds of Europe or Mexico City; the California idyll was a permanent part of the ranch myth: a private bucolic world, an escape—the Ranch House.[27]

The 1946 book by *Sunset* and May included a selection of architects from Seattle to San Diego. There was a wide range of variation in the book's definition of the Ranch, from Gardner Dailey's strikingly contemporary house with a slanting roof to Hugh Comstock's cozy cottage-like Ranch House. Clarence Mayhew's sophisticated 1937 Manor House in Orinda, and William Wurster's 1927 vernacular Gregory Farmhouse were also included. The book can be seen as a cross section of a style that was still evolving. The text does not champion the suburban lifestyle of family rooms and open plans, though such plans are included. Master bedroom suites are sizable and private, a small world with a large bath and private outdoor terrace—a luxury mass-production homes did not include until the 1990s. The framework of the Contemporary Ranch House can be seen, but the modern aspects of the designs are not pronounced or promoted. The kitchen—the utilitarian realm of servants—was blended into the main house in response to social trends; but the utilitarian surfaces of brick and unpainted wood were polished and made respectable for the middle class, while retaining the romance of a rugged rustic kitchen. Of course, the addition of dishwashers and refrigerators made the rustic appearance easier to live with.

These were custom homes, neither mass produced nor affordable. However, their comfortable middle-class image, broadcast through *Sunset*, helped shape the taste of the customers walking through the model homes of developers such as David Bohannon, John Long, and Fritz Burns.

Custom Ranch Houses After the War

As civilian buildings were made possible after the war, custom-home architects once again built one-story suburban homes. High-art architects still found the Ranch House a fertile subject, while other architects found it popular among clients across the country. The Ranch may have begun as a regional style, but it quickly became a national style; Contemporary

Tract homes, c. 1952, Phoenix, Arizona. John F. Long, developer. Open houses allowed prospective homebuyers in Arizona's growing economy to see the latest house plans and features. The single-story Ranch was the most popular type, especially for Easterners moving to work in Phoenix's growing electronics industry. Though simplified, ornamental elements such as the board shutters on the house on the left clued visitors to the Ranch character of the design.

Contemporary Style tract home, c. 1955, Phoenix, Arizona. John F. Long, developer. White gravel roofs serve to ease the effects of the intense Arizona sunlight and give a contemporary look to this Ranch.

Tract house, c. 1954, Community St., San Fernando Valley, California. Variations on the Traditional Ranch House included farm house and barn elements, with barn-red siding and gambrel roof forms.

Ranch Houses could be found in Vermont and Cape Cod Ranches could be found in Pasadena, California; architect Harold J. Bissner's 1949 house in Pasadena, clad in wide weathered shingles, boasted flower boxes beneath the windows and the steeper roof of the Cape Cod, but it nonetheless had the open plan of the Ranch.[28]

Entire neighborhoods of large, custom-designed Ranch houses by local architects and builders could be found on commodious lots in Phoenix's citrus district and the neighborhoods of the San Fernando Valley's Northridge area, not far from modest tract subdivisions.[29] The Ranch's democratic spirit, its solid and practical plans, and the pleasure of the outdoor life made it one of the most widespread residential types, both in custom and mass produced homes, in the twentieth century.

Yet, its emergence was something of a surprise to some in the architectural establishment. "Blinded by the angular International Style," wrote *American Home Magazine* editor William Hennessey in 1949, "few of us were conscious of another movement that was then taking place on the Pacific Coast. There a number of promising young architects were developing a new kind of building, a style that shows every indication of becoming as characteristically American as the early Cape Cod house. They were taking the old Western ranch house as a basis, and bringing it up to date, using materials honestly and logically. Native woods were left natural to show their intrinsic beauty of grain. Plans were allowed to ramble since rooms were all placed on one floor. Windows were located to gain the widest and most effective views of the surrounding country; not, as before, simply to produce symmetry of exterior wall design. . . . Since they are postwar-built, economy forbids them to ramble too far; consequently a more flexible plan has been evolved, one which makes one room do the work of two or three."[30]

William Wurster

William Wurster, who had helped define the Ranch House before the war, was still interested in its formal possibilities. Along with the sophisticated San Francisco townhouses and peninsula estates he designed—influential models for a generation of postwar architects—Wurster and his partners,

The Ranch House at the Peak: The Tract

Tract home, c. 1956, Phoenix, Arizona. John F. Long, developer. Pacific Palisades Ranch House resident and General Electric spokesman Ronald Reagan promoted GE's newest electric kitchen appliances at a special GE Home, built by John F. Long, who stands at right. Stovetops, built flush into the kitchen counters, and dishwashers constituted some of the most effective and direct uses of modern technology in the improvement of the life of the average family and were made available in Ranch tract homes like those Long built.

Tract home, c. 1953, Phoenix, Arizona. John F. Long, developer. Though usually built of the concrete block more available in Phoenix than the wood-stud frame homes found in California, these Ranch tract homes featured wood porches, board-and-batten veneer siding, and shallow gabled roofs to convey the Ranch House image.

Harwell Hamilton Harris

Another contributor to the prewar Ranch style was Harwell Hamilton Harris, who built the 1945 Ingersoll Demonstration House in Kalamazoo, Michigan, which, noted David Gebhard, "conveys a hint of Wright, as well as of the California ranch house" in its broad, earth-hugging roof.[31] Gebhard's wife Jean Murray Bangs introduced Harris to the Greene brothers in 1948, and their influence was immediately reflected in Harris's Clarence Wyle House in Ojai and his 1948 Ralph Johnson House in Los Angeles. With wide, feathered eaves, exposed rafters and a ground-hugging profile, these designs strengthened the ongoing Ranch House aesthetic in Harris's work.

Moving to Austin, Texas, in 1951 to head the school of architecture at the University of Texas, Harris found the broad Texas landscape sympathetic to his evolving designs. The 1952 Thomas Cranfill House in Austin is pointedly angular with a pop-up clerestory window. Long and low like a Ranch House, with a board-and-batten wall facing the street, the house opens up to the garden through glass walls.

The *House Beautiful* Pace Setter House Harris designed with his students in 1954 is a classic Contemporary Ranch House. Built at the Dallas State Fair grounds, the redwood and yellow-pine house was later moved to a residential area. It was an inherently suburban design, long and sprawling, which paid careful attention to the automobile. "There is one fact of modern life: the front door is where you park your car. . . . the garage itself [should] be as formally inviting as a reception room of a great old mansion," wrote Joseph Barry in presenting the house in the magazine.[32] Harris's "Motor Reception Hall" (the garage) used the same stone floor as the courtyard garden adjoining. The courtyard with pool and planting was suited to the hot Texas environment before air conditioning became widespread. As in his own Lowe House and in Cliff May's houses, each room had an outdoor extension, carefully concealed from the street with planting or fences. The kitchen was a separate room, but the living room, study, courtyard, and dining room flowed together. Sliding doors acted as partitions to make the space flexible. A corridor ringed three sides of the courtyard (see pp. 146; 186; 198).

Theodore Bernardi and Donn Emmons, continued to design rural and suburban Ranch houses in the spirit of the 1940 Reynolds House near Gilroy and the 1947 Kenneth Mortsolf House in Atherton, which featured a prominent gabled roof over a plan with bays and wings. The plan reflected the simplicity of Wurster's work, which possessed a studied care to the large windows and pop-out bays that gave subtle interest to the design. The plain board-and-batten walls and modest detailing echoed smaller tract homes of the same era. Other noteworthy Ranch designs from the Wurster office are the small 1946 M. P. Davison House in Fresno (designed by Theodore Bernardi), and the 1956 George Pope House, a sizable two-story in Madera with a second level porch around the entire house, based on yet another rural working-ranch vernacular form.

In this house, as in Wright's and Wurster's, the Ranch House shows its full potential as high-art architecture. The spaces of the house flow indoors and out in an easy and successful manner. The informality of the suburban lifestyle mirror the flowing, asymmetric composition of the forms. Harris fully explored the artistic potential of suburban architecture, which—to suburbia's detriment—was ignored by most high-art architects.

O'Neil Ford

O'Neil Ford also returned to the themes of Ranch architecture in the decade after World War II. Though his designs shared the simplicity and natural materials of the vernacular precedents he loved, they also revealed Ford's exploration of Modernism. His 1946 McNeel House in San Antonio (with Gerald R. Rogers) is a low-slung house that shapes itself to prevailing winds and light; shaping houses to local conditions was a primary lesson Ford learned from vernacular architecture (see p. 102).[33]

Frank Lloyd Wright and His Followers

Since designing Broadacre City in 1935, Frank Lloyd Wright demonstrated his interest in suburban design and planning. Several architects influenced by Wright explored the design of the low-slung single-family suburban home. John Lautner's 1947 Schaeffer House in Glendale, California, set on a suburban street, is the iconoclastic architect's version of the Ranch House: a boldly articulated horizontal board wall wraps around the yard and the house, while an energetically angled wood-raftered roof floats over the sprawling plan. Schweikher and Elting's 1949 Herbert Lewis House in Park Ridge, Illinois, showed the strong links between the Ranch and Usonian house: the L-shaped plan turned glass walls to the garden side; simple gabled roofs with wide eaves formed open-scissor truss ceilings on the inside.[34] Their house for Mr. and Mrs. W. Russell Scargle in Glenview reflected similar ideas.[35] Even in the harsh Chicago climate, an open carport was a feature of the front door and entry, as with May and Choate's tract homes in California.

Corbin Palms, 1953, San Fernando Valley, California. Palmer and Krisel, architects; Alexander Construction Company. The first large development by this prolific architectural firm, Corbin Palms' Contemporary Ranch houses turned walls to the street, and opened up to back yards. Free palm trees were given as an incentive to buyers. The tract is on the west side of Corbin, near Victory Boulevard.

Wright himself continued his evolution of the Usonian house in a way that made it difficult to tell if he was boldly leading (his interpretation) or running to stay at the front of the crowd. The flat-roofed Usonian of the 1930s gained a gabled roof with wide eaves in many of his postwar houses. Wright may simply have been returning to his own aesthetic invention of the wide-eave roofs of the Prairie Style houses of forty years earlier; but clearly other architects, including Harwell Hamilton Harris, were already using the forms long associated with the Ranch House.

Wright's 1951 Zimmerman House in Manchester, New Hampshire, is one of the best examples of his absorption of the Ranch type. In the last decade of his life, when he was more famous than ever, Wright continued to spread the concept of the single-family contemporary home through constant publicity in popular magazines and professional journals. Wood-plank ceilings, red brick pillars and fire-places, wide-gabled roofs emphasizing horizontality, open floor plans, and easy access to outdoor patios paralleled the Ranch House of the average suburban neighborhoods. Other Wright houses of this period used dramatic geometries in plan and silhouette to put the avant-garde Wright imprint on the designs, but the broad shingle roof remained dominant, linking the designs to the Ranch houses of the period.[36]

Cliff May

Although Cliff May could have continued to repeat his earlier, picturesque style after the war, he instead chose to evolve his designs under the influence of the Modern sensibility. The irregular, painterly compositions were rationalized with larger, simpler gabled roofs that almost touched the ground, and exposed post-and-beam structures.

Cliff May's 1963 Eshelman • Bemis House in Rolling Hills, like many Jones and Emmon's designs for Eichler, turned its high-gabled profile to the garden and filled its broad face with glass (see p. 216). Yet the picturesque May touches, seen in heavy carved Spanish doors and furniture, baroque wrought-iron chandeliers, and abundant pot shelves softened the stark modernity; this was still a Ranch House. By the 1950s, May was also regularly using sliding-aluminum frame-glass doors to connect indoors to outdoors; these

often replaced the fixed living room windows of his earlier houses.[37] Likewise, May's kitchens were large and informal, designed to be living spaces, not the hidden functional realm of servants. Breakfast rooms and sunrooms were combined with rustic brick-floored cooking areas. These rooms were also inspired by the vernacular and informal working-ranch house (but not the hacienda, where traditionally cooks were relegated to out buildings or the courtyard to reduce on heat, odors, and fire danger in the main house). The barbecue was, however, selected as a worthy element to be repeated in the Modern Ranch House—and promoted extensively by *Sunset* magazine.

In 1958 a second May-*Sunset* book appeared, devoted exclusively to his designs. By the time May's *Western Ranch House* was published, he had moved from wood stud construction (rendered to look like thick-walled, hand-applied adobe) to post-and-beam construction—a method both historic and modern, blurring the lines between the two. In the 1930s, May began designing in a romantic historicist mode, as seen in the 1946 book; in this new book, he adapted the Ranch House to contemporary lifestyles of the 1950s. In his 1957 experimental house, also included in the book, May took this conceit so far that many of the interior partitions and closets, set on casters, were actually movable; the space could be reconfigured in almost any way desired. Never before had the Ranch House met the future so boldly, but even after getting a fair amount of publicity, May's experimental house did not, after all, catch on.

With its progressive attitude, *Sunset* was aware of the concepts of Modernism under discussion—and controversy—in the architectural profession in the 1940s and 1950s. "The Magazine of Western Living" consciously linked the Ranch House to Modernism. Function was the primary mantra of Modernism, of course, and the ease of tending, cooking, and living in Ranch houses was often used as a justification for the style. The historical imagery in the Ranch House's moderate Modernism was an indisputable part of its appeal, but one which *Sunset* and May distanced themselves from rhetorically. "Good ranch houses do not need wagon wheels," they assured their modern readers in the 1946 book, but they were not as rigidly doctrinaire as were most Modernists:

model A-1

Top: Rendering, 1951, San Fernando Valley, California. Palmer and Krisel, architects. Model A-1 is a rendering of Palmer and Krisel's first tract home design. They went on to design over 20,000 Modern housing units in Southern California, surpassing the number built by developer Joseph Eichler.

Opposite: Corbin Palms, 1953, San Fernando Valley, California. Palmer and Krisel, architects; Alexander Construction Company. The architects refined their post-and-beam building system to speed construction and reduce costs. The insulated ceiling panels were pre-painted; windows were nailed to the outside of the structure instead of requiring framing. The living room featured balanced light from clerestory windows.

Following spread: Rendering, 1951, San Fernando Valley, California. Palmer and Krisel, architects.

Left: Ranch house tract, 1961, Woodland Hills, San Fernando Valley.

Right: The Coronado/Plan 305C, Lakewood Plaza, c. 1955, Long Beach, California. Aldon Company, developer. A typical Southern California Ranch House subdivision of the mid-1950s, Lakewood Plaza provided larger, more upscale homes compared to those in nearby Lakewood. It is on Los Santos Drive, near Studebaker.

"Ranch houses have been able to absorb everything our machines have produced without losing character."[38] The enchanting fact was that the garage for the cars could also look like a barn for horses. The historical overtones could not be easily justified in modern theory, but the pleasures of memory were obvious to the popular audience. Just as Hollywood movies blurred the line of historical time, so could Cliff May in the service of creating effective architecture.

The Tract Ranch House Goes
Upscale and Contemporary

"The California ranch-style house had become an American prototype," wrote Wayne Whittaker in the October 1958 *Popular Mechanics*. As summed up by historian Kevin Starr in 2002, the Ranch House meant "simplicity of design, flexibility of indoor-outdoor spatial arrangements, the convenient re-siting of family rooms adjacent to kitchens, the use of glass walls and skylights, the integration of heating, ventilation, and electrical systems, the concern for landscaping, the ease of

maintenance."[39] These features were seen in both ultramodern Case Study houses and many tract Ranch houses as well.

Near the minimal Ranch houses of Lakewood, built for workers at the nearby aircraft plants, developer Ross Cortese built Lakewood Rancho Estates in 1954, a smaller, slightly more expensive tract of modernized Ranch houses designed by Cliff May and Chris Choate. With open plans and exposed post-and-beam structures (instead of Lakewood's boxy rooms), the homes attracted buyers who were middle management and engineers at the aircraft plants. Also nearby, the Aldon development company built Lakewood Plaza, which offered four bedrooms and up to 1,350 square feet of home. These were Traditional Ranch houses in ten different exterior styles, from the Valley Provincial model with diamond pane windows to the Friendly Hills with its board-and-batten siding.

This range of Ranch houses evolving in the tract-home market in the 1950s reflected the style's acceptance and flexibility in a growing and prosperous era. Beginning in 1950,

The Ranch House at the Peak: The Tract

developers like David Bohannon explored larger (and more profitable) tract homes with different features and styles—explorations that would eventually make Ranch the most popular housing type of the era. Consumers wanted more choices. Breaking from the minimal FHA standards, square plans became rectangular among the spacious possibilities of sprawling one-story Ranch houses—regularly featured to the public in the pages of *Sunset, House Beautiful, Better Homes and Gardens,* and other magazines targeted at homebuyers.

Reentering the civilian market after the war, David Bohannon finished Hillsdale and continued to perfect his methods, maintaining "his own complete architectural staff and land planning department," according to one newspaper.[40] The assembly-line construction process he and Marlow-Burns pioneered before the war was now being identified as the "California Method."[41] The public recognized this building phenomenon as a wonder of the age alongside jet planes, atomic energy, and transistor radios.[42] Though the "California Method" was a convenient label for this innovation, and

though many home builders across the country were figuring out the common formula for mass-production building, "Big Dave" Bohannon got a fair share of the press—and credit. In April 1946, *Fortune* magazine featured his California Method of operative building; and in 1949, the *Wall Street Journal* put him prominently on the front page.

"It's a myth to think the mass builder saves much on costs. There's probably not 5% difference between his operating costs and that of the small builder and that's absorbed by overhead. But the mass builder can have the best architects and other specialties and his house will give better value," claimed Bohannon.[43] Inherent in the idea that a house could be stamped out by an assembly line like a car was the inference that a house was a mass commodity, not a custom design. Such thinking undermined the traditional role of the architectural profession, which widely believed that quality design required individual attention. "The merchant builders had for some years been acquiring great tracts of land, and housing had become an industry—

Left: Eichler Homes, 1955, Terra Linda, California. Anshen and Allen, architects; Joseph Eichler, developer. Eichler sought to bring good Modern design to the mass-production home industry in the 1950s and 1960s. His houses are noted for open plans, elegant post-and-beam details, and convenient, spacious links between the backyard and the interior.

Right: Tract home, 1948, Panorama City, California. Wurdeman and Becket, architects; Kaiser Homes, developer. Postwar housing developments, like this one, used modern construction, organization, and marketing methods to provide affordable single-family housing. The mass-production methods and minimal Ranch House design pioneered by developers Fritz Burns, David Bohannon, and a few others before World War II bore fruit in the tremendous number of new houses consumers clamored for.

an intensely competitive one in which the architect was bypassed by the developer. In place of good architecture the developer depended on the loaded kitchen and bathroom to sell his houses: countertop ranges, refrigerators, dishwashers, and garbage disposals were finally included in the price of the house, along with a sunken tub and expansive tile work," wrote Esther McCoy.[44]

Bohannon tested the contemporary Ranch House market with the *House Beautiful* Pacesetter House in 1950, built in Hillsdale. Though Bohannon was probably aware of competitor Joe Eichler's recent Modern tracts in nearby Sunnyvale (by architects Anshen and Allen), Eichler was nowhere near as prominent as Bohannon was in 1950. More likely Bohannon's own appreciation for Modern design (seen in his Gardner Dailey-designed home) prompted him to explore the possibilities of Modern styles for a new product. Certainly his connections with the prestigious *House Beautiful* magazine, edited by powerful tastemaker and editor-in-chief Elizabeth Gordon, and the Pacesetter series (begun in 1948, it also featured houses by Harwell Hamilton Harris and other respected designers) were good publicity. Bohannon's designs were the first merchant-builder homes to be selected for the series. Designed by architect Edwin A. Wadsworth, in conjunction with Germano Milano, and landscaped by Thomas Church, the model was strikingly Modern with exposed post-and-beam structure, planes of wood and glass, open carport, and a large gabled roof with wide eaves. The same team designed two other models, Contemporary and Traditional Ranch, whose styles reflected similarities.[45] Like the ultramodern dream cars displayed by Ford, GM, or Chrysler at auto shows to test public reaction, the Pacesetter design attracted customers' attention, while favorite features could be applied to the more conventional models, which most homebuyers preferred to purchase.[46]

One Bohannon tract in San Mateo attracted the attention of the professional architectural journal *Architectural Forum* in October 1951, indicating a higher level of design. Bohannon's 1951 Mayfair Heights neighborhood in San Jose is an even more significant example of a Contemporary Ranch tract. The houses have the horizontal form and asymmetric massing of the Ranch; one story, single-gable

roof, set parallel to the street, sporting an inset front-door porch supported by a four-by-four column. They were cleanly detailed, with an ornamental screen to shelter a bedroom window from the street. Although the garage faced the street, the key evolution in the plan was the living and dining rooms that formed a single room from front to back, with sliding doors leading out to the back yard. Even without overt historical decorative clues, this contemporary design was accepted as Ranch at the time. "One of the Bohannon architects inspecting the job told visitors that the new home could be called a ranch-type house somewhat modified with a touch of California-Colonial design," reported a local newspaper.[47]

During the 1950s, Bohannon's in-house architecture department was headed by architect Mogen Mogenson; his designs ranged from well-conceived Modern, to Contemporary and Traditional Ranch House.[48]

The Changing Role of Architects in Tract Housing

Architects responded differently to the new surge of mass-housing development. Some were appalled at being sidelined by the rapid construction methods and commodification of the American house. Others were excited by the rationalized systems being explored in real-world construction, and saw this phenomenon as an extension of Modernism itself.

Developers utilized architects in different ways. Some, like John F. Long in Phoenix, had their own in-house design departments that developed most of their house plans, facades, and community plans. Other large developers had ongoing relationships with independent architecture firms, but held a firm reign on the direction of the models. Smaller developers likewise hired architects or plan services to design their models. These architects worked in both Traditional Ranch and Contemporary Ranch styles.

A few architects, however, took a more aggressive stance and carved out a new role for themselves. Two Southern California firms, Edward Fickett and Palmer and Krisel, were particularly successful, working with dozens of developers. A third partnership between Cliff May and Christian A. Choate created yet another innovative way for architects

Top, left: Tract home, c. 1954, Cord Avenue, Downey, California. Mid-range tract Ranch House models achieved a relatively common form across the breadth of suburbia. A comfortable compromise between modern lines and Traditional materials and symbols, the L-shaped plans included an attached garage, creating a car drive at the front of the house. Board-and-batten siding was frequently used, but in broad planes that used it as a textural veneer and an appealing traditional image, not as structural system.

Top, right: Tract home, c. 1954, Downey, California. Barn-red paint and ornamental elements (note the dovecote, left) created another picturesque variant of the Ranch House style. Numerous gable ends, applied to the facade, suggest the Ranch's sprawling wings, even in this relatively modest tract home.

Bottom, right: Tract home, 1957, Westwood Oaks, San Jose, California. Mogen Mogenson, architect; David Bohannon, developer. Large developers such as Bohannon included Contemporary Style Ranch models mixed in with Traditional ones. The post-and-beam structure and clerestory windows were also seen on Palmer and Krisel, Fickett, and May and Choate designs.

Bottom, left: Tract home, 1957, 3633 Cody, Westwood Oaks, San Jose, California. Mogen Mogenson, architect; David Bohannon, developer, A simpler formality is used in this tract model. In another Westwood Oaks model, the garage was detached from the house and brought forward, creating a private forecourt to complement the backyard. That design (based on survey results from a woman's magazine on their favorite house features, said architect Mogen Mogenson) won a 1957 Citation award from *American Life Magazine*. Cliff May and Chris Choate also used this configuration to create more usable outdoor space.

Tract home, 1957, Anaheim, California. The range of Ranch House styles included more fanciful interpretations, bringing scrollwork fascia boards echoing styles from Swiss and fairy tale traditions. Though clearly a Ranch House, its inspiration lies someplace other than the romanticized historicism of Cliff May designs; the proximity of Disneyland, opened in 1955, may help to explain it. Its scale, composition, and ornament nonetheless express a cohesive, assured aesthetic.

Opposite: Tract home, 1957, Anaheim, California. Another dimension of Ranch architecture can be seen in this Anaheim tract. By exaggerating the scale of the roof, the house hugs the ground; overscaled brackets maintain the scale, drawing on the California tradition of the dollhouse or fairy tale architecture of Hugh Comstock and Walter Yelland. While the minimal Ranch houses of Panorama City reduced ornamental elements to the minimum that still conveyed the Ranch image, this house exaggerates those iconic elements.

to participate in the housing boom. Though architects' services were more expensive than a plan's services, many developers saw the value in what these architects provided.

The "Cliff May Homes"

A distinctive version of the Contemporary Ranch House was introduced in 1952 in Cupertino, California, by a key figure in the development of the Ranch House—Cliff May with architect Christian A. Choate.[49] May's ease in accepting both a historic sense of the Ranch House and the facts of a modern lifestyle, made his designs more relaxed than those of some Modern architects who were ill-at-ease with any hint of historical influence.

Well aware of the postwar demand for new and affordable housing, May and Choate created a small version of the May Ranch House (see p. 132).[50] Slimmed and rationalized by a modular post-and-beam construction, the houses succeeded in being both Modern and Ranch. May-Choate homes used prefabricated windows, and doors and panels to fit into the module of the structural posts. The most extraordinary aspect of the design is its generous use of the small sixty-foot suburban lot: three distinct and usable outdoor spaces are created. The living room's glass doors and windows spill out onto the entry patio (sometimes sheltered between house and detached garage); the kitchen has its own patio along the side yard; and at least one bedroom has a door out to a backyard.

The houses are small—an average of 950 square feet— but the indoor and outdoor spaces are arranged in a more open manner than the minimal FHA-standard houses seen in Lakewood and Panorama City. Using low partitions to define kitchen from living room, the small house appears more spacious as the overarching roof unites the interior space. The first houses in Cupertino had rough-sawn wood beams on the ceiling; later improvements used smooth, painted board. Board-and-batten or rough-sawn plank exteriors link the designs to the Ranch tradition, but their broad dimensions turn them into textural planes—a Modern conceit. Wide-railed glass doors and sliding windows give these houses a simple, clean scale.

Notable was their manufacturing and distribution system. Marketed as "Cliff May Homes," the partners designed each

model and specified each element of the wood structure and fixtures; these specifications were then franchised by region to builders, lumber yards, or other parties who fabricated the pieces of the house and either sold them to builders or developed tracts themselves. A 1954 advertisement showed franchises from California to Louisiana. They also patented the design and building system; each piece of wood was stamped with a "Cliff May Homes-Patent Pending" mark. May successfully sued the Bristol Development Company, the Federal Construction Company, and architect William Bray in 1955 for infringement of copyright plans at Bristol Manor in Santa Ana.[51] The idea of architects owning and legally defending their intellectual property rights was unusual at the time, a byproduct of the commodification of the Ranch House.[52]

Edward Fickett, Architect

Edward Fickett's designs used simple forms that were both clearly modern and designed for easy, economic construction. His models are primarily rectangular, though he also carved away creatively for distinctive entries and porches. In post-and-beam construction, only four structural posts at the center of the plan were needed to support the weight of the roof; this allowed interior partitions to be freely placed to create functional rooms.

The 1,000-home Sherman Park subdivision was a typical 1953 Fickett tract, developed for Ray Hommes in the San Fernando Valley, the site of much of his work. As *House + Home* reported, the tract sold 251 houses in two weeks, while a conventionally designed tract nearby sold only 70 in two months.[53] Models ranged from 940 to 1,145 square feet with an open carport; the living room and dining area formed an L-shape with glass walls wrapped around an outdoor porch facing the back yard. Sherman Park homes sold for $10,200 to $11,400.

Hommes was a typical Fickett client. A builder of apartments and commercial buildings before World War II, he honed his building skills with military contracts during the war. Decreasing house sales in 1949 on his Cape Cod, Spanish, and Colonial models lead him to Fickett, who convinced the forty-eight-year-old developer of the advantages

Edward Fickett

Architect Edward H. Fickett (1923–1999) grew up with sympathy for the builder's perspective because he had worked summers as a carpenter for his father and grandfather who were builders. "Coming from a family of contractors has taught me to respect the builder, subcontractor, and other members of the building team," he told his fellow architects.[54] It helped him bridge the mutual suspicion between architects and builders whom, he explained in 1961, "are somewhat reluctant to consider commissioning an architect because they have heard stories about the successful architect being 'temperamental,' 'doesn't consider construction costs,' 'is a dreamer,' or 'has no real knowledge of public taste.'"[55]

Fickett was a protégé of Sumner Spaulding, the architect of both Rolling Hills Ranch homes and Case Study House #2 (1947, with John Rex), who encouraged him to become an architect.[56] He studied at both the University of Southern California and Art Center School. After three years with the Navy's Civil Engineering Corps, Fickett began his own practice in 1947. It was a time when "the big-time merchant builders . . . were having no trouble at all selling mile upon mediocre mile of conventional bungalows. Burgeoning postwar Los Angeles was so hungry for houses it asked only that they have roofs and a little plumbing," reported *House + Home* in 1953.[57] But by 1950, tracts were beginning to move up-market, and developers realized that the architect's imprimatur was, at the very least, a helpful sales tool. "Architect-designed" became a featured line on many tract billboards and newspaper ads.

Seeing an unexploited niche, Fickett began a campaign to convince builder-clients that architect-designed home models would improve their product and their profit. In this closeknit building community, a client of Fickett's, who was a savings and loan president, put him in touch with a builder whose sales were slowing. From 1947 to 1953, he designed 18,000 houses for a dozen builders.[58] By 1953, *House + Home* magazine reported that he was making "$100,000-plus a year from merchant builders alone" in his ten-man office in Beverly Hills.[59]

Yet, Fickett served only a narrow part of the building industry; he reported that only one in ten builders who he interviewed with decided to hire him. Those that did (such as Palmer and Krisel), saw a clear value in modern features and construction that justified the added expense of hiring an architect.[60] Fickett would prepare a site plan locating each house and infrastructure, gain FHA and VA approval (and make any necessary changes for their requirements), coordinate with subcontractors, create full working drawings for each model, submit drawings to necessary agencies, supervise construction of the first four or five houses, coordinate colors, regulate mode furnishings, and research new materials and methods. With furnished models and landscaped lots (Fickett and Hommes's Meadowlark Park in the San Fernando Valley was landscaped by Eckbo, Royston and Williams, who designed landscapes for several Case Study architects), the creation of a total picture of the contemporary lifestyle was made possible, and this in turn helped sales. According to *House + Home*, Fickett's designs and Hommes's success with Contemporary Ranches spurred other developers to do the same. According to Dave Slipher of the Fritz Burns organization, "The Fickett-Hommes success in Sherman Park gives us heart to speed up our own contemporary styling. . . . It is a forward step, and deserves looking into by builders, although not too many have had to face it yet."[61]

of good architecture—not only regarding sales potential of contemporary design, but in the polished plans, new eye-catching features, and efficient organization of construction. With Fickett designs, Hommes's production increased from 200 to nearly 2,000 houses per year in his work between 1949 and 1953.

From 1948 through the 1960s, Fickett's designs evolved from Traditional Ranch to Contemporary Ranch. An early design in North Hollywood for Coronet Construction Company was a simple gabled rectangle with shutters and shingled roof; as he convinced builders to become more confident with contemporary designs, the traditional ornament of the Ranch—horizontal wood siding, exposed rafter ends—was abstracted. The lines of the house became simpler, seen in well-proportioned fascia lines, and the geometric framing of windows and doorways. Screen walls were modern compositions of open concrete block or louvered wood slats. Trellises over entryways or carports were smoothly integrated into the roof. Ceramic-covered rock enwrapped the low sloping roof (an average Ranch House had one-to-two inches in a twelve-inch slope).

Palmer and Krisel, Architects

Esther McCoy's opinion on architectural design is worth listening to; she helped to revive the reputation of R. M. Schindler, and she translated the ideas of the Case Study houses into indelible words. Thus, her observation that a Palmer and Krisel work in a subdivision "gives distinction to tract houses," should carry some weight.[62]

It can be argued that architects Dan Palmer and William Krisel fulfilled many of the goals of the Case Study Program—namely, to bring modern spaces and building technology to the mass housing audience—more successfully than did any of the houses actually included in the program.[63] But as mass-produced houses, Palmer and Krisel's designs grappled with more hard-nosed building industry constraints than did any Case Study house cushioned by custom-house budgets.

Corbin Palms, Palmer and Krisel's first large development, is a key example of the Contemporary Ranch tract.[64] Set in 1953 in Canoga Park for developer George Alexander

Meadowlark Park, 1952, San Fernando Valley, California. Edward Fickett, architect. This tract near the corner of White Oak and Saticoy boasted landscaping by Modernist landscape architects Eckbo, Royston and Williams. Board-and-batten siding, a staple of Traditional Ranch House design, is used in this Contemporary Style Ranch House as a textural plane that catches sun and shadow.

The Ranch House at the Peak: The Tract

Tract home, 1960, Clawson, Michigan. As the Ranch House spread in tracts across the country, it adapted to local building conditions. The style of this minimal Ranch House, of brick and capped with an American Colonial gable end, is Colonial. The form, however, with a low-pitched roof, horizontal lines, and an asymmetric arrangement of windows and doors, is Ranch.

in the fast-developing San Fernando Valley, the long, casual volumes, capped by a low-pitched roof and wide eaves, create private suburban homes with clean modern lines. Turning a mostly windowless facade to the street (there were clerestory windows), echoing the solutions of Harwell Harris and Wright's Usonian homes, the houses open to the backyard through glass walls and french doors (sliding doors were still too expensive); in addition, most rooms had outside doors.[65] Because the post-and-beam structure on a concrete slab eliminated bearing walls, partitions dividing kitchen from living room stopped short of the ceiling. The high ceiling gave the interior a broad spaciousness.

Conventional tracts like Panorama City and Lakewood were cut-and-fit wood stud and plaster buildings, and their architecture reflected a structure of boxy-like rooms and windows that resembled square holes cut out of the walls. Palmer and Krisel, like May and Choate, developed a distinct modular post-and-beam structure that was flexible and rapidly constructed. Krisel had been trained in modern-

system buildings by Cal Straub at the University of Southern California; he applied that knowledge to the assembly-line construction method of the building industry. As they designed, Palmer and Krisel streamlined the structural pieces and details with consideration for the ease, speed, and simplicity of construction. "We tried to eliminate the [on-site] cut and fit stuff," explains Palmer.[66]

The system was conceptually simple: based on a thirty-two-inch module, all lumber lengths could be predetermined and precut, eliminating time on the job taken up by sawing. Beams and lintels were pre-painted, which eliminated even more labor. Instead of the two-by-four studs set out every sixteen inches in standard construction, a four-by-four post was set every sixty-four inches around the perimeter of the house. A four-by-six lintel rested on top of the posts. A high-ridge beam ran down the central length of the building, and four-by-six rafters at thirty-two inches on center connected it to the outer walls. Celotex—a new lightweight composition board of processed wood twenty-four inches wide, eight feet long, and two inches thick—formed the pre-finished plank ceilings. The roof was typically covered with asphalt and colored rock.

Windows and doors (fabricated especially for this system by suppliers working with Palmer and Krisel) were applied to these spacings; kitchens were laid out to fit into three such modules, bathrooms into two, bedrooms into four, and living rooms into five. Windows were nailed directly onto the outer surface of the posts, eliminating time and labor in setting and trimming frames in the traditional manner. So simple was the installation that inexperienced (and therefore less expensive) framers could be hired and instructed.

With this system, a house could be built in ten to twelve days. The houses did not meet all FHA requirements, so all financing was through conventional private sources; Palmer and Krisel firmly believed that FHA standardized specifications wasted money compared to their non-standard modular system. After a house was built, the owner could qualify for an FHA loan. "We got into the market to prove that a system could work and could be profitable," says Krisel. "We sympathized with our builders," says Palmer, "like [Eichler architect] Quincy Jones did." They found something satisfyingly cre-

Tract home, 1953, Birmingham, Michigan, Frank Gobel Corp., builder. Compare this house to Frank Lloyd Wright's Cheney House on page 25. The influence of the Prairie Style can be seen in this and many other Ranch tract homes from the 1950s. It is seen in the brick walls, hipped roof, stone coping, wide eaves, and clustered windows. The form, however, still qualifies as a Ranch House. Though slightly larger and orienting its long side to the street (to emphasize its size and leisurely Ranch House sprawl), this small Ranch is similar to the Raised Ranch, a Chicago building type that evolved from the Chicago bungalow of the 1910s and 1920s. Typical of the Midwest, they include basements, where California Ranches frequently did not.

ative in the process of building, in the challenges of building in huge numbers, in rubbing against the restraints of budgets, organization, and the culture reflected in market forces.

The Evolution of Ranch House Characteristics

The evolution of the tract Ranch House plan is not precisely linear. Innovations (such as family rooms) were gradually accepted, and eventually defining elements (such as the placement of the living room-family room on the rear of the house and accessing the rear yard through sliding doors) were generally accepted. Prior to this point, the arrangement of bedrooms along the front of the house, or the side, or the rear, could be found in various examples throughout the period. At Rollingwood and Panorama City the kitchen was placed at the back of the house for privacy, giving mothers a view of the backyard where children played. In Lakewood, the kitchens were often on the front, with the same justification.

The backyard was an integral part of the Ranch. In larger custom homes, it would have been designed by Thomas Church or another noted landscape architect. Plantings enlarged the apparent spaciousness of the lot; irregular lines emphasized the rolling hills of the prairie landscape, not the strict geometries of formal garden design. The backyard was redefined as a place of planned recreation, and pools and childrens' play equipment were often included. Entertaining was equally important; barbecues, large trellises to shelter dining tables, and other features opened the middle class backyard to a luxurious life—essentially turning the outdoors into a truly usable outdoor room.

Since the Prairie Style house, modern architecture had evolved an open concept of living space. As home life became more informal, kitchens became less utilitarian and more like other rooms in the house, blending with dining rooms and living rooms to form the family room. The baby boom shifted the focus of home plans on family life. According to developer John F. Long, the open plan originated with the desires of the homebuyer: "It didn't all happen at once . . . Early on we had a kitchen and a place to eat in it if you were lucky. With the family room it allowed you to make the house more open."[70]

The Ranch House at the Peak: The Tract

Palmer and Krisel

Dan Palmer (1921–) entered the architecture school at New York University in 1937, where maverick Modernist Edward Durell Stone was his design critic, and he worked for Morris Lapidus. He met his mentor, Frank Lloyd Wright, while helping him set up an exhibit of his work at the Museum of Modern Art. In 1945, he moved to California to work for Victor Gruen; among the projects he worked on was Milliron's, Gruen's landmark suburban department store in the Marlow-Burns development of Westchester. At Gruen's office in 1946 Palmer met William Krisel, who was then still an architecture and landscape design student at USC. Palmer left Gruen's office in 1947, after receiving his architecture license, to form his own firm; Krisel joined him in 1949 as a design associate, and then as partner in 1950.[67]

William Krisel (1924–) entered architecture school at the University of Southern California in 1941, and then enlisted in the U.S. Army. He spent the war in China on General Joseph Stilwell's staff; born in Shanghai, Krisel spoke the language fluently. Resuming his studies after the war, he graduated in 1949 and obtained his license in 1950.

While in school, he would pass Baldwin Hills Village (Reginald Johnson, Wilson and Merrill, Robert E. Alexander, architects; Clarence Stein, planning consultant) on his way to USC every day. Just five years old at the time, Baldwin Hills Village was celebrated as a well-conceived medium density housing project; with two-story linked units situated around common green space, it followed in the footsteps of Radburn and other suburban housing solutions from the previous decade.[68] Another suburban development Krisel was well aware of— along with most other young architects in Los Angeles—was the Mutual Housing Association community of 1947. This was the result of a group of young professionals with an interest in progressive design (among them architects A. Quincy Jones, Whitney Smith, and Wayne Williams) who pooled resources and created the Crestwood Hills development—including a community center—in the hills of Brentwood. Jones designed many of the original houses for the project, but in 1950, Krisel contributed with his own designs.

As partners, Palmer and Krisel began by designing custom homes in Bel Air and Brentwood, where in 1950 they evolved the modular post-and-beam system they would later use in their tract homes. In 1951 they built their first small tract of ten homes in the San Fernando Valley. The homes sold out quickly, attracting attention. The 247-home tract of Corbin Palms in 1953 for the Alexander Construction Company was their first major housing project.[69]

Palmer and Krisel carved out their own building industry niche by becoming linchpins in the building development process, especially for less experienced developers. In the boom years after World War II, investors from other fields (known colloquially as "cloak and suiters") wishing to enter the potentially lucrative housing industry sought out Palmer and Krisel. The partners offered a one-stop service to put together an entire package: designers, builders, bankers, suppliers, sales force, and general experience; they built 20,000 units of housing by 1958 in Southern California. "Some clients came to us because they liked our designs. Others liked the designs because they were popular, and also liked the cost cutting methods that meant a profit," says Palmer.

Their successful tracts and ideas gained national attention. *Architectural Forum* and *House and Home* published frequent articles on the firm, noting their good designs, intriguing building systems, and their commercial success. Palmer and Krisel spoke at housing conferences across the country and, as a result, received commissions in Florida, Texas, El Paso, Salt Lake City, Las Vegas, Phoenix (for John F. Long), and elsewhere. Developers from around the country vacationing in Southern California would visit Palmer and Krisel tracts to see where the trendsetting California market was heading.

Their partnership was dissolved in 1960, though both continued to use the valuable Palmer and Krisel name for five years before carrying on individually. Krisel continued building in Riverside and San Diego counties; Palmer covered Los Angeles, Ventura, and Orange Counties—he later continued in commercial design, and became a developer himself. Krisel continued in high-rise condominiums and office buildings.

Corbin Palms, 1954, San Fernando Valley, California. Palmer and Krisel, architects; Alexander Construction Company.

Tract home, 1955, Bloomfield Hills, Michigan. The Ranch House is an architectural type defined by its suburban site and its horizontal form. It can embrace many styles, however, including Contemporary, Traditional, Spanish Colonial Revival, and, in this case, American Colonial Revival.

Suburbia and the Tract Ranch House

The Ranch House became the favored housing type as Americans moved to the new suburbs after 1945. Phoenix, for example, attracted new plants for rapidly growing aerospace and electronics firms like Motorola. When executives returned to their Eastern headquarters, they brought back brochures from John F. Long Homes to show employees the spacious, sunny, modern, and affordable homes they could own when they moved to the Southwest. Likewise, when transferred employees visited Phoenix to search for homes, they could visit the "John F. Long International Home Show" or "John F. Long's Futurama." The new tract openings were shows veering on spectacles, like the unveiling of the new model cars every fall at car dealerships. Huge temporary billboards plastered with festive advertisements funneled home buyers into a demountable sales center that could be moved from site to site.

From the beginning of his tract building career, Long applied the Ranch style, which he defined simply as a one-story home with board-and-batten siding and a porch across the front. Many of his customers were from the Midwest, and the Ranch's novelty, its association with the desert West, and its spacious plan made it their most popular model. "California is the trendsetter," said Long, "The Midwest had no ideas."

Long's largest development opened in 1955: Maryvale in west Phoenix, with 25,000 homes on 2,000 acres, which was aimed at first-time homebuyers. Los Angeles architect Victor Gruen, known for his role in defining the modern shopping mall, planned Maryvale with shopping centers, parks, landscaping, and community centers. "It was helpful to have someone of their caliber to see what to look for over the long term," said Long. Maryvale's initial homes echoed one of the simplest vernacular Ranch House precedents, adapted to the mid-century consumer and construction techniques. With walls of concrete block—which were common and sensible in the desert because of their insulation properties—the rectangular homes included a shaded porch along the street side. Carports or single-car garages were included under the long gabled roof.

The Ranch House at the Peak: The Tract

John F. Long

John F. Long (1920–) "was touted all over as the world's most efficient builder," said Ned Eichler, son of one of his California colleagues.[71] Long nurtured his organization from one house, which he built in 1947 for himself and his wife after getting out of the Army. This Phoenix native was a self-taught builder; raised on a farm, as a child he would tear down an old barn and build a new one. Clearly, construction came naturally to him. He built his first house virtually by hand, figuring out how to save time, be more efficient, and how to make it "easier and interesting" for carpenters. "I did everything the hard way," he notes, referring to that first house in which he used only a handsaw.

Through 1948 and 1949, Long built about a dozen custom homes this way, one at a time, closely observing and analyzing the building process with each one. Beginning in 1949, he started on his first tract with thirty-two lots and three-bedroom houses going for $6,600. "It was something I liked, a challenge. I didn't think there would be a housing boom." He wanted to build larger houses to earn more profit and did so later in 1949. But when the FHA came out with a $7,000 ceiling for qualification, purchasable with a low 10% down payment, smaller (1,100 or 1,200 square feet) houses became more saleable, and Long followed the trend by focusing on lower-priced models.

As had Bohannon and other developers before him, Long broke down the construction process into distinct steps. As his business grew, he continued to visit building sites everyday, searching for ways to improve the building process, and communicated with his supervisors each step of the way—from concrete, framing, sheet rock, and so on.[72] He noticed that the details he paid attention to also interested his employees, and he encouraged them to suggest improvements to the operation. If one crew framing walls figured out ways to speed their work, that would put pressure on the next crew—say, framing the roof—to figure out ways to do their job more efficiently; the most efficient crew of the month would be rewarded with a dinner, though Long saw to it that the honor was evenly distributed. "If you cut five dollars here, do that ten times, and multiply it by five hundred homes," you improved your profit line, he explained. "I always had an open mind going in, looking for ways to cut costs and improve product," he said.[72]

Regionalism and the Ranch House

In the late 1940s, the Ranch House was central to one of the primary debates over the future of Modernism in the architectural profession. Even though Ranch was rarely discussed in high-art circles, some of the style's primary architects, including William Wurster and Harwell Harris, were involved in these debates.

The main issue at hand was the place of regional influence on architecture. A symposium at New York's Museum of Modern Art in 1948 ("What Is Happening to Modern Architecture") took up the debate. The issue came down to wood, with which the Regionalists of the American West were identified. On one side, wood was championed as human, while machine imagery was censured as cold, formal, and inhuman. On the other side, machine imagery was championed as precise, objective, and ideal, and wood was condemned as sentimental.

There was some confusion about what, exactly, was taking place in Western architecture during the late 1930s and 1940s. Journalist Talbot Hamlin wrote in 1939: "It is this feeling—that the house is the thing, and not its style—which is recreating the domestic architecture of California and at least in part, of Texas. These houses I saw are definitely American, unlike those to be found anywhere else in the world, and not because of any vaunting nationalism, any attempt to impose on refractory form an intellectually chosen style, but because their architects, working simply, have created houses above all else. O'Neil Ford's Texas buildings . . . are as direct and as simple in their approach as the California work. It would seem, therefore, that here we are dealing, not with a mere local and accidental development, but rather with a growing trend, originating perhaps in California and gradually spreading eastward, a trend toward a kind of house design which is modern in its results because it is modern in its purposes, and not because its architecture has some fixed prejudices as to what was modern in style."[73]

Wurster's continuing interest in domesticity—his patios and porches, his wide sheltering roofs and pleasant Thomas Church gardens, his warm wood paneling and residential scale—also singled him out for criticism. Far from daring, he

John F. Long, developer of numerous tracts and communities in the Phoenix area, approached the mass production of houses as a process of constant refinement to increase speed, reduce expenses, streamline methods, and respond to the changing desires of the public. Long built as many homes as did the Long Island-based Levitts, the postwar developer mentioned in many mid-twentieth century architectural histories. Still, Long's contributions (and that of dozens of other developers across the country) have been underplayed in comparison to their innovations and impact.

seemed middlebrow, though not as much as Cliff May, who rarely figured in high-art debates of the times.[74] To many, Wurster's approach seemed undemanding. Expressing disappointment, historian Henry-Russell Hitchcock asserted that, "With Wurster there seems to have been no conversion. . . . in which the stylistic virtues, such as they were, of the early work have gradually been lost without any comparable achievement in a positively new form." But he also admitted, "There is much that I do not understand about building conditions on the [West] Coast."[75]

This ambivalence and antagonism toward Western architecture lead curators such as Arthur Drexler and Hitchcock to ignore the Bay Area (and Wurster in particular—not to mention the Ranch House) in their exhibits and books for MOMA in 1952. However, Elizabeth Mock, Henry Wright, and George Nelson included many Wurster houses—including many Wurster Ranch-style homes—in their postwar books of modern housing examples.[76]

Outside this academic debate swirled another in the popular magazines, a debate in which the Ranch House figured prominently. Elizabeth Gordon, editor of *House Beautiful*, vigorously and vociferously supported American regionalism, including the Ranch House. This raised controversy, as demonstrated by William Jordy's comment: "The regional aspects of modernism, unfortunately led to flag-waving, as the vulgarization of any kind of regional idealism always does. Thus an 'American' modern was suddenly proclaimed in the pages of consumer magazines. And its 'humanism' and 'individuality' were implicitly, and sometimes overtly, contrasted with the 'mechanistic' and 'communal' (even 'communistic') of early European Modernism."[77]

While these debates spanned the late 1930s through the 1950s, the Ranch House continued its development. It thrived through this period, though out of the spotlight of the high-art architecture world.

Custom Ranch Houses in the Late 1950s and 1960s

The Ranch House continued to evolve as a form into the 1960s. The architecture profession was moving in different directions, reassessing its Modern roots. By the end of the decade, even the stalwart housing industry would give up

the Ranch as its favored type. But for the architects who had long used its informal, flexible vocabulary, the Ranch was still alive and well.

One such supporter of the style was Harwell Harris, who drew richly on the Ranch form in houses in Big Spring, Texas, for Dr. and Mrs. Milton Talbot in 1959, and Dr. and Mrs. J. M. Woodall in 1958 (see pp. 186; 198). He also drew on Craftsman and Wrightian influences for his residences; in fact, the single-story Ranch form was only one of many he mastered. In 1955, Harris left the University of Texas and moved to Fort Worth to focus on his architectural practice. In 1962, he moved to Raleigh, North Carolina, even farther from his California roots, to teach at the School of Design at North Carolina State University. Throughout his teaching career, he continued to design houses. "The 1964 Lindahl House in Chapel Hill was close to the California ranch house in plan; like Ramona's Marriage Place in San Diego, it was a U-plan around a court. Lindahl was a Californian, so client and architect spoke in a shorthand both understood," wrote Esther McCoy.[78] The low-pitched hipped roof of the Lindahl House had wings spread out over the landscape like an errant pinwheel.

Meanwhile, Texan architects continued to draw from and adapt the specific Ranch traditions in that state. O'Neil Ford gained publicity for his Regional Modern designs. His 1959 Dale Carter House in Tulsa, Oklahoma, was selected as a Hallmark House in 1963 and published in *House and Garden* magazine. The 1959 Hugh Fitzsimmons House on San Pedro Ranch near Carrizo Springs, Dimmit County, Texas, carried on the long-low simplicity of Ranch homes, featuring large wood framed windows.[79] Ford's office, like Wurster's, grew in size and scope as he designed university campuses, factories, and large complexes, but he always designed homes as well. His office became a major training ground for Texas architects.

Charles Dilbeck was another Texas architect who balanced traditional styles with modern adaptation, showing a fresh approach that included the Ranch style; examples included the R. E. Griffith House in Dallas and the Julian Meeker House in Ft. Worth. Like with his contemporaries, Dilbeck's initial experiences in the building industry involved a grass roots job as a teenager learning the nuts and bolts

The Ranch House at the Peak: The Tract

(or studs and nails) of builder housing. He worked for a Tulsa lumber company where he helped adapt stock house plans for builders to use. In 1929, he opened his own practice and moved to Dallas.

Where Williams and Ford looked at the stone indigenous home of east Texas—square stone structures that were more typical of small towns than the wide open plains—Dilbeck "was attracted to a different type of indigenous architecture, the sprawling Ranch houses of the Panhandle and West Texas," wrote David Dillon. Texas, like California, has long and varied vernacular traditions, and architects of the mid-century mined all the potential sources. "I was the first to develop Texas Ranch houses," claimed Dilbeck in 1979. "Others had done city-type Texas houses, but not ranch houses. These usually started out as plain log houses, which were built onto as the family grew. The log house became the hog pen and so on. If the owners made a lot of money, they'd build a Colonial or a gingerbread up on top of a hill, and the original ranch house would become a second or intermediate house. But if you look closely you can almost always find the original log house in there somewhere."[80]

Dallas architect John Staub's Dan Harrison Jr. Ranch reflects this low, sprawling character. The additive look over time was aesthetically appealing, especially to those architects (such as May) wishing to paint a rustic picture. This style contrasted with the use of abstract forms and plane walls that Modernist's like Ford and Wurster incorporated in their designs. Both approaches, however, contributed to the evolution of the Ranch House style.

The place of the Ranch House in American architecture is still not widely discussed. There are few other examples in twentieth-century history where modern technology has been applied so directly in order to provide decent mass housing, and so the Ranch House represents a victory for Modernism. It also represents the triumph of place and individuality over worship of the machine, for Ranch drew on eminently popular plans and styles, rich with memory and myth in the popular culture. The ambiguities that make up the Ranch style, built on the fabrication yard used during construction, show it to be a moderate Modernism. 👢

Ranch home, 1958, Troy, Michigan, R and C Builders. Devoid of Traditional Ranch ornament, this large custom Contemporary Ranch in the Midwest emphasizes the ground-hugging lines of the Ranch.

Wagner House (originally May house), 1939, Los Angeles,

The Ranch House Today: A Tour

4

This page: Though not the inventor of the Ranch House, San Diegan Cliff May spread the gospel of the Ranch House through scores of designs and hundreds of articles in the pages of many popular magazines. His houses in the early 1930s reflected the adobe tradition of Southern California haciendas, contrasting with the wood vernacular buildings of Northern California that inspired Stockton-native William Wurster's Ranch House designs in this period. Wood doors on the street wall open to this entry court, with the front door at the right. The windows show May's original horizontal panes. The wing at the opposite end was extended by a later owner for a bedroom; the casually angled wings make additions blend smoothly without affecting the original concept. May often included a long pot shelf/bench, in the foreground; deep-set door frames also reflected the appearance of adobe construction.

Opposite: This living room looks out onto the landscaped fountain court. The horizontal window panes are typical of May designs in the 1930s, though the original fixed window has been replaced with French doors that repeat the original lines.

Lilypond House   Cliff May, Designer   Los Angeles, California, ca. 1935

Top: Beyond the street wall, the house consists of several wings, set at irregular angles, wrapping around courtyards. The living room wing is at left, the bedroom wing is to the right. Porches and wood posts recreate the hacienda image. Many rooms open to the outside—a traditional hacienda plan that the suburban Ranch House reflected even before Modern architects adopted the same strategy. **Bottom:** Two traditional aspects of the hacienda interpreted in this house (in Mandeville Canyon, site of numerous May houses) include red tile roofs and a long wall with small windows turned to the street. **Opposite:** Exposed wood ceiling beams and a corner fireplace are elements borrowed from the Hispanic haciendas of the southwest. But May adapted those historic forms: while haciendas were usually rectilinear and U-shaped, May angled his walls to create a more romantic picture and to open to the landscaped gardens. They also evoked a pleasantly irregular, rustic, hand-crafted quality to the designs in sharp contrast to the machine lines of Modern housing. Flooring includes wood planks and large clay tiles.

Lilypond House

This page: By the late 1930s, the Ranch style had become as acceptable as Tudor, Colonial, or Classical for Southern California custom homes (as well as for the large tracts of several developers.) Many architects had mastered the elements of the style. Lutah Maria Riggs was one, and this four-bedroom ridge-top home in Rolling Hills can be considered a classic example of the Traditional Ranch. Originally built for C. V. Knemeyer, it displays an artfully unstudied placement of splayed wings, as if additions had been built through the years as needed. The living room is at the left. Opposite: A covered porch connects the garage with the kitchen door. Brick foundation walls rise to the window sills, a frequent identifying detail of the Traditional Ranch.

Knemeyer · Mills House   Lutah Maria Riggs, Architect   Rolling Hills, California, 1939

Opposite: A bedroom wing (not original) features wood beam ceilings and plank walls without molding or trim–a rustic detail that suits the Ranch style. The French doors open onto the pool terrace. **Top:** The windows of the remodeled kitchen look out to the front entry, an informal feature typical of the casual lifestyle expected in Ranch houses. **Bottom:** Glass doors make the living room airy and light; one side opens to a brick terrace, the other side to a covered porch. Like the young families who made the Ranch popular in the 1950s, current owners Marc and Lisa Mills and their large family find the Ranch a more convenient, casual home than the current crop of suburban mini-mansions.

This page: The living room wing's covered porch with wood post, exposed rafters, and board-and-batten walls are typical features of a Traditional Ranch House, rendered by Riggs with comfortable proportions. It could be a set for any Western movie at the Saturday afternoon matinee; in fact it was designed as an upscale house for a well-to-do family. The large master suite, a paneled den and bar, formal dining room, tennis courts, horse barn, and orchid house—as well as well-crafted wood details—demonstrate how this rustic style became suitable for an upper-middle-class lifestyle.

Opposite: The house is an idealized Ranch set on a breathtaking five-acre site on the top of the Palos Verdes peninsula. The living room's stone terrace (not original) looks out in one direction over the Pacific Ocean, in the other toward the Los Angeles basin. Rolling Hills was planned as a community of second homes, underscoring the growing importance of middle-class leisure time in twentieth-century architecture.

Kneymeyer • Mills House

This page: Actor Robert Wagner now lives in the first of three houses Cliff May built for himself over the years in Riviera Ranch, his first planned community. A friend of May's, Wagner asked the designer to remodel and add to the house after he moved here in 1983. Wagner had known the area since childhood, however; after his family moved to Los Angeles in the 1930s, Wagner's father had stables at the polo fields directly across Sunset Boulevard (the site is now home to a high school). The wide covered passage leads to an inner car court, with the stables on the left and the front door on the right. Wood grill over the window is another pictur-esque Cliff May detail. **Opposite:** The landscaping has grown lush, making the house blend further into the setting. May used this house to promote the Ranch House concept (and his career) in the pages of several national magazines and his books with *Sunset Magazine*; modern media spreading such infectious images struck a chord in the mass audience. May's influence was due at least as much to his Ranch propaganda in magazines as to his actual buildings, which often served as set dressing for the photos in his magazine articles.

May ★ Wagner House   Cliff May, Designer   Los Angeles, California, 1939

Opposite: Like Rolling Hills, Riviera Ranch is the idealized Ranch House neighborhood that ordinary tracts emulated. True horse country, most houses here have their own stables, and riding trails line the winding lanes instead of sidewalks. **Left:** Windows and window seats line the hall, or *corredor*, of the bedroom wings. Several bedrooms have their own walled courts. May adapted the hacienda's exterior walkway that linked the rooms by enclosing it. Some rooms incorporated the hall into their space, enlarging their size. **Right:** The remodeled kitchen maintains the rustic flavor of the original. **Following spread:** In his remodel, May changed out the original living room windows looking out on the spacious backyard for sliding aluminum doors, once they became available. The wood-beamed ceiling along the room's edge marks the *corredor*, the perimeter circulation path through the entire house; the wood beams recall the exterior walkway of a hacienda from which he derived the idea. Echoing the hand-crafted techniques of adobe construction in the living room, May typically used curving bull-nose corners on doorways and mantles, as if workers had smoothed the adobe by hand.

Left: The original four-car garage was enlarged as a stable, with dovecote, in the additions May designed for Wagner after he moved here in 1983. **Right:** Like most Ranch houses, the image of this house is low profile and unpretentious, hidden behind walls and unobtrusive gates. **Opposite:** Another addition by May for the stable includes a tall hayloft. **Following spread:** Cliff May's picturesque sensibility—taking conventional elements and exaggerating them to dramatize the rustic or historic character of ranches—is seen in the thick walls with rough plaster revealing the adobe textures; in deep dramatic reveals for windows and doors; planters and bench shelves creating a base for the building; and massive chimneys rising from roughly textured shake roofs. This carefully composed image was part of the Ranch House's appeal, and was repeated (though rarely with May's flair) in thousands of suburban tracts using the Traditional Ranch style.

May • Wagner House

Left: One of Texan O'Neil Ford's first designs, for artist Jerry Bywaters in 1929, was an almost perfect replica of the modest rural homes he had admired on many car trips along Texas backroads. But by 1946 he had been introduced to Modernism, become acquainted with William Wurster, and had (like Wurster) evolved his ideas about the Ranch House. Designed with partner Gerald Rogers and built for Amy and William McNeel, the house is now the residence of architect Jay Pigford. Ford appreciated the way vernacular working-ranch houses responded to the intense San Antonio climate; in this design he creatively updated that sensitivity in a passive solar house that used thick brick walls, orientation to the breeze, clerestories, and ceiling fans to keep the house comfortable. The wing shown here was added in the 1970s by Ford's office. **Right:** Ford designed two pairs of doors—one solid for winter, one louvered to allow breezes for summer—for the front entry. **Opposite:** This living area was added in the 1980s by Ford's office, Ford, Powell and Carson. The Contemporary Ranch House lines were continued.

McNeel ★ Pigford House   O'Neil Ford, Architect   San Antonio, Texas, 1946

Left: Brick walls and steel-frame windows are original features of the bedrooms. Architect Jay Pigford, who has lived here for four years with his family, admires Ford's honest use of materials. **Right:** The simplicity of the details—no base boards, plain trim—made housekeeping easier and echoed the rustic character of Texas working-ranch houses. This kitchen fireplace warms the small dining area. **Opposite:** Now that the house is air conditioned, the original screened porch seen here has been glassed enclosed. Angled toward the prevailing summer breeze, it scooped air into the clerestoried living room at the heart of the house. Originally, jack-knifed glass doors between these two rooms lifted overhead to allow air to flow through in the summer, or closed to retain warmth in the winter.

This page: A prolific designer, Cliff May designed scores of custom homes large and small over a half century. The Evans House is typical of many, with a casual, open plan and easy access to the out of doors. The small porch is a later addition. **Opposite:** May's designs placed several wings, usually one-room deep, at oblique angles to fit the site. Future additions could be smoothly blended at the intersections or off the ends of wings. This seemingly unstudied layout also created small private patios that used the property more effectively. French doors have replaced the original aluminum sliding doors.

Evans House   Cliff May, Designer   Los Angeles, California, 1947

Left: The master suite has a sitting room and a private patio. Additions were designed by Peter Choate, son of Chris Choate, May's partner in his tract-home projects. **Right:** Plank ceilings refer to the rustic character of historic working-ranch houses. **Opposite:** The traditionally furnished living room is illuminated with a metal skylight down its ridge—a striking modern feature not found in historic working ranches, but a signature design element of May.

Evans House

Top: May's planned community, Riviera Ranch in Sullivan Canyon, permits stables. Their presence lends veracity to the Western myth every Ranch House embodied: a prairie home and the independence of the wide-open spaces. Most tract developments suggested that myth in their style, their layout, and other trappings. They accomplished this, with great popular success, despite the fact that in most tracts one house was cheek by jowl with its neighbors. Of course, the Ranch House was never meant as a historically accurate replica; it was a modern invention that drew on historic Western architecture and cultural mythology to shape the modern house. **Bottom:** Working ranches were set in a productive countryside; landscaping for the Ranch House was equally informal and useful. Naturalistic groupings of trees, foundation planters to tie the building to the ground, and circle drives to accommodate the auto were some of the formal conceits often repeated in Ranch House landscaping, themes going back to Frederick Law Olmsted's design for Riverside, Illinois, in 1869. Noted Modern-era landscape architects such as Thomas Church and Garrett Eckbo often contributed to the Ranch designs of both custom designers like May and Wurster, and tract architects like Palmer and Krisel. **Opposite:** Though an interior corridor links the living areas to the bedrooms, they can also be reached outside through the garden, increasing the blending of indoors and out.

Evans House

This page: The 1948 Spier House is part of a small one-block tract of half-acre lots built by the Gibraltar Construction Company. Developers as large as California's David Bohannon or Texas' Frank Sharp were a minority; most builders were much smaller in scope. Sunken lawn lined with brick indicates that it is a citrus subdivision; indeed it was surrounded by citrus groves until 1958. The original orchard irrigation system that flooded the groves is still used to water the trees and landscaping twice a month with six inches of water. **Opposite:** Constructed of concrete block (used in Phoenix almost exclusively until the 1970s), the shallow gable roof and front porch still followed the wood ranch prototype. The board-and-batten bedroom addition to the left blends with the original rectangular house.

Spier House Gibraltar Construction Company   Phoenix, Arizona, 1948

Top: With the living room on the front, the kitchen and bedrooms look out on the backyard. Not all Ranch houses had sliding glass doors to make outdoor access easy; this tract turns a utilitarian block wall with steel sash windows to the rear. Special block with curved corners, however, frame the windows. **Bottom:** The classic Ranch House roof line was used in this simple but ample Ranch home. Carport is to right. Current owner Scott Spier and his family have lived here since 1990, finding it easy to add on to the original two bedroom/one bath as their family grew—a characteristic of the Ranch. **Below:** As seen in this original newspaper advertisement for the Spier House's tract, tiled kitchens, steel sash windows, and attractive financing were as much a part of the appeal of Ranch architecture as the ingenious floor plan and sturdy construction.

Left: The original living room was turned into the dining room shortly after the house was built. Arched doorways are original.

Right: The substantial ashlar stone chimney brings a Traditional Ranch look to this early tract home. Plank ceilings contrast with modern metal casement windows.

This page: A magnificent custom home so unobtrusive that it seems to grow out of its hillside site, the Gimbel House is a classic Ranch design. It accommodates its residents—actress Jennifer Warren and director Roger Gimbel—without commotion or pretense, with dignity and ease. The brick wall of the kitchen's Dutch door is something of an anomaly in the timber-frame building; it almost seems a fragment of a ruined mission around which the house was designed. **Opposite:** The long rambling garden side of the house shifts and angles, allowing private entries to both bedrooms and the large living room. The house does not truly have a front door, a testament to the ultra-casual Ranch ethic; entry is through the kitchen, or through the large wood-framed sliding doors of the living room.

Gimbel House Cliff May, Designer   Los Angeles, California, 1950

Left: The master suite is almost a cottage in itself. Its own porch opens onto the pool, hedged in for privacy. **Right:** The living room's massive stone fireplace, set in an inglenook, evokes high country lodges in Montana and Wyoming. The cinematic aspects of May's designs are clear, going beyond the appeal of his designs to many Hollywood stars, including Gregory Peck and Robert Wagner; May recognized intuitively the profound effect of mass media on architecture and taste. In the 1950s, high-art critics claimed that the Ranch was inappropriate anywhere outside the West, believing that buildings must reflect their site. This failed to recognize a major shift in perception spurred by the media age. If a John Wayne movie was as popular in Maine as in California; why shouldn't a Ranch House? High-art Modernism's insistence on ideological purity and machine imagery did not take into account this consequence of the modern technology of cinema, which brought the world into everyone's lives. **Opposite:** The kitchen of the Gimbel House preserves May's original design intent, a rare occurrence as most have been remodeled. The rustic elements are more than picturesque; there are roughly sawn planks and brick surfaces and yet the room is warm and welcoming—both painting a picture and working functionally.

This page: The living room's heavy-timber construction introduces a grand scale made intimate by the checks in the wood and iron straps banding members together. The inglenook is to the right, the large sliding glass doors on wood frames to the left. The house was designed for an architect on May's staff.

Top: A simple garden gate welcomes visitors from the car court to the main lawn. **Bottom:** The house slowly reveals itself to visitors, as seen in this view inside the gate. Ranch houses did not need to impress, however, and it saves some of its surprises to be revealed later. **Opposite:** At the master suite, the large home seems no more than a modest Ranch House, with a simple gabled roof and board-and-batten siding.

Gimbel House

This page: A variation on the Contemporary Style Ranch House found in Houston that includes a second story, a concession to local design guidelines. The diverse history and large population of Texas created an architectural community sufficient to create many different responses to the Ranch. **Opposite:** The concrete frame house with glass and brick infill has a distinctive window treatment of fixed and horizontal panes. The living room is at right.

Ford House   Lucian Hood, Jr., Architect   Houston, Texas, 1953

Top: In this custom house design, a modern composition of wood paneling and stone mantle echo the clean lines of the exterior.
Bottom: Clerestory windows and glass walls bring the light and views of outdoors into the interior of the house—a key element of Ranch House plans. **Opposite:** The backyard includes naturalistic Ranch House landscaping, including free-form pool and barbecue.

Ford House

Left: On the sloping site at the foot of the San Gabriel Mountains, this Ranch uses the topography to create two stories and terraced gardens.

Right: Stripped of historic-themed details such as board-and-batten siding, this design reveals the essential form of the Ranch House type. The long front porch leads to the front door, with the kitchen and family room on the left; the open plan does not require a formal sequence of spaces. Wood rafters are exposed overhead, but steel columns instead of wood support the beam in this Contemporary Ranch. **Opposite:** The garden extends the kitchen space, just as the deck extends the living room. The lack of attention to Ranch houses in most architectural history books distorts our understanding of twentieth-century Modernism. Dogmatic critics deemed the Ranch House, with its explicit or implicit use of historically themed imagery (from Old West to Colonial to Spanish) an impure architecture. Yet the architects and developers who refined modern materials and construction methods into systems so functional and affordable that hundreds of thousands of decent housing units could be created served the interests of Modernism more successfully than a handful of houses known only to the readers of history books. The Ranch House challenges the way we have understood and written about twentieth-century Modern architecture.

Dadd-Griffith House Altadena, California, 1953

Left: The rustic ashlar fireplace and chimney of Traditional Ranch houses (see the Spier House in Phoenix, p. 115) is given sleeker modern lines in this Contemporary Ranch. **Right:** In the 1950s, homeowners who were not at ease with the severe lines and metal surfaces of a Modern house could enjoy a relaxed blend of progressive and traditional design in the Ranch House. The furnishings in this living room are Modern, but they suit the exposed wood beams and broad stone wall. **Opposite, left:** The kitchen decor mixes different eras. Updated cabinets mingle with a mass-produced kitchenette table and high-art molded-plastic chairs from the 1950s. **Opposite, right:** Ribbon windows, high on the wall, balance light in the family room. A simple wood table reintroduces the rustic Ranch-style theme.

Dadd-Griffith House

This page: Though known mostly for his luxurious custom Ranch houses, Cliff May also plunged into the mass production of Ranch tracts. With partner Chris Choate, May created a regular building system suited to mass production, but also retained popularly appealing Ranch-themed elements such as board-and-batten siding. Like the Craftsman bungalow, the popular Ranch House cut across social class to become a truly democratic phenomenon in the 1950s, a home fit for factory workers and movie stars, for future presidents and for rock-and-roll stars; Elvis Presley and his parents moved into a Ranch at 1034 Audubon Drive in Memphis in 1956. The Ranch House could be found in a range of sizes and imageries for every rung of the social ladder. May and Choate's tract designs were slightly larger, slightly more expensive, and more adventurous architecturally in their open design than those in the enormous Lakewood, California, development nearby. Lakewood Rancho Estates appealed to mid-managers and engineers at nearby aerospace plants (some of whom still live in the neighborhood) who saw the models at Studebaker and Spring streets; the same plants' factory workers often bought the more affordable minimal Ranches found in Lakewood. **Opposite:** The simple post-and-beam construction system May and Choate developed is revealed in this remodeled interior. It differed from the standard stud-wall construction used more generally in tract houses, such as those in nearby Lakewood. Modular windows and doors were designed to fit into the regular rhythm of the structural posts.

Burgeno House Cliff May, Designer; Chris Choate, Architect; Ross Cortese, Developer Long Beach, California, 1954

Opposite: The flexibility of the post-and-beam structure and its large open spans permits easy remodeling. The kitchen, at left, was originally separated from the living room with a low partition; now a counter divides the spaces. The wealthy built luxury custom-designed Ranches in suburban enclaves such as Arcadia, California, and Bloomfield Hills, Michigan. But the significance of the Ranch as a social phenomenon in the 1950s lies in the fact that blue-collar laborers were suddenly able to aspire to middle-class homes and lifestyles for the first time in history on such a widespread basis. Developers such as Fritz Burns intentionally sought social and vocational diversity in his communities—though, pointedly, not racial diversity. Though small (usually 900 to 1,200 square feet), May and Choate's designs made superb use of the outdoors, in the best tradition of the Ranch House. Glass doors allowed access from different rooms to patios on each side of the house.

This page: This enlarged bedroom carefully continues the height, sliding wood-frame windows, and exposed-beam ceiling of the original. Original floors were linoleum tiles, while original ceilings were Celotex panels. The roof was tar paper and rock.

This page: John Entenza invited Harwell Harris to design a Case Study house; though Harris declined, he would have been one of several of the avant-garde architects associated with the program who also designed Ranches. This fact highlights the strong similarities between Modern and Ranch, even though the suburban style was not generally embraced by the high-art architecture community devoted to European Modernism. In Harris' work, however, the artistic dimension of the Ranch is thoroughly revealed. **Opposite:** Harris often ended his tall gabled spaces with a large window framing the natural view. The original owner was David Barrow, an associate in Harris' Texas office. Susan Gould is the current owner.

Barrow ★ Gould House Harwell Hamilton Harris, Architect   Austin, Texas, 1955

Top: The flowing open plan of the Ranch House is fully realized in this design. Harris uses glass and well-proportioned spaces to both unify the space and create distinct areas. **Bottom:** The dining area off of the living room feels as much outdoors as indoors. **Opposite, left:** Harris used gabled forms that proved appealing to the homeowner who did not like the flat roofs of Modernism—even though he and William Wurster were both criticized for their use of regional sources and popularly appealing materials. **Opposite, right:** Stone fireplace echoes the hand craftsmanship and local materials used in historic working ranches.

Barrow • Gould House

This page: The Sensing House is a textbook example of the Traditional Ranch House. Many wings ramble easily over a large site, clothed in simple board, shingle, and brick materials; compare its roofline to the Gregory Farmhouse on page 26. It is a large custom home, and its materials are luxury ones but the details and ornament do not show the extravagance of wealth. The landscaping is naturalistic. It conveys the cowboy myth of independence, self-reliance, and simplicity. **Opposite:** East of Needles, this style of Ranch was called the *California Ranch House.* It uses a formal vocabulary selected from historic working ranches: horizontal wood siding, shake roofs, large brick chimneys, windows divided into small panes, and a low brick foundation. The amoeba-shaped pool reflected the freeform shapes of Modern art translated by the pool fabrication industry. **Following spread:** In the warm Arizona climate, the enclosed porch, or Arizona Room, on the left forms a transition from the shady interior to the bright exterior. Substantial walls of glass are rendered, in Ranch architecture, in stretches of small glass panes.

Sensing House   Allied Builders   Phoenix, Arizona, 1955

Top: While many Ranches use open plans that blend living, dining, and family rooms, this is more formal, devoting an individual room to the dining room. **Bottom:** This remodeled kitchen with paneled wood cabinets and cove molding is also formal, rather than rustic. The Ranch's moderate Modernism permits a flexible range of responses to changes. **Opposite:** Appropriate furnishings for Ranches vary. The traditional furnishings of this living room are closer to the historical taste of prosperous owners of actual working ranches than to the mid-century Modern furnishings of the Dadd-Griffith House seen on page 130. If they could afford it, nineteenth-century ranch owners brought furniture, pianos, chinaware, and other luxuries at great expense to their homes in the wilderness.

Sensing House

This page: Harris' earliest designs, including the 1933 Lowe House and the 1935 Fellowship Park House, borrowed from Japanese architecture. The Antrim House two decades later also returns to this inspiration. **Opposite:** Besides Traditional, Contemporary, American Colonial, and Spanish Colonial, another subcategory of Ranch houses is Oriental. In the hands of architects other than Harris, the references are usually more overt: gable ridges end in upswept peaks, front doors are framed in circular moon gates, and ornamental motifs for shutters, screens, and railings are derived from Japanese or Chinese design (see 23057 Oxnard, Woodland Hills, and 850 Orange Grove, Arcadia, California.) Harris, however, draws on the understated proportions and elegant textures of Japanese buildings. Note how the paired doors at right open the entire face of the house and neatly stow themselves against the wood posts. **Following spread:** The house opens gracefully to the garden, a theme in both Ranch and Japanese architecture.

Antrim House Harwell Hamilton Harris, Architect   Fresno, California, 1956

This page: The front entry passes by a landscaped court. The front door is at the center of the photo. **Opposite, left:** Long corridors linking the public spaces with the bedrooms are common in one-story Ranch houses. Harris uses light and woodworking to make the corridor a distinct place in itself. **Opposite, top:** With its massive block of brick, the fireplace conveys a sense of weightiness that recalls Frank Lloyd Wright, another influence on Harris. So does the ornamental wood trim visible on the ceiling. **Opposite, bottom:** Lowered soffits, left, and shoji screens are other Japanese elements that Harris used. Coming full circle, Japanese design influenced Charles and Henry Greene when they designed their Craftsman-style homes, predecessors of the Ranch House.

Antrim House

Top: The front of the house, though carefully designed, reveals little of the inner home. Like both Wright and Spanish prototypes, Harris often turned a plain wall to the public street, and focused his houses on the private backyard. **Bottom:** The broad gabled roof and anchoring chimney identify this design as a Ranch House, though the generous floor-to-ceiling glass openings avoid the small framed windows of the Traditional Ranch. **Opposite:** With its gently sloped roofs and horizontal lines hugging the ground, this house expresses the archetypal relationship of the working-ranch house to its site. The house merges with the land and landscaping, rather than standing apart in contrast, as do both Classical and Bauhaus-Modern design.

Antrim House

This page: The Hanley House was originally built for Patrick and Bea Haggerty. Patrick Haggerty was a co-founder of Texas Instruments, for which O'Neil Ford was designing a daringly Modern plant as this house was built. Opposite: The house reflects the best aspects of Ford's work; there is an nonchalance about the shapes and lines that matches the Ranch House's modesty, but look carefully and Ford's extraordinary care for detail is obvious. Ford, his brother Lynn (an artist), and the Haggertys traveled to northern Mexico to select brick and stone for the project.

Haggerty ✶ Hanley House   O'Neil Ford, Architect   Dallas, Texas, 1956

This page: The large open-plan house comfortably accommodates art. This room shows both the simplicity of vernacular architecture and the craftsmanship of design and execution that is required to achieve that simplicity in a present-day house.

Left: Bedrooms have convenient access to a sheltering porch and the gardens. **Right:** The kitchen continues the same brick and wood craftsmanship seen throughout the house. **Opposite:** The carved doors, dramatically lighted by a skylight, were carved by Lynn Ford, O'Neil's brother and frequent collaborator.

Left: Double beams run down the gabled roof's ridge. The right wall becomes glass. **Right:** The brick end wall and asymmetrical doors appear to have come from a vernacular barn. Though he used such elements directly in his earliest designs, Ford's design aesthetic evolved over the years as he incorporated such sources into his concerns for modern construction and prevailing climate. **Opposite:** The composition of forms, textures, and colors in Ford's architecture create a setting for the clients' art and life. In this and other houses, Ford sought an appropriate suburban residential architecture that drew on regional character and modern building methods.

This page: Dry desert peaks, dusty desert landscape, split rail fence: if you think that the Miller House's setting looks like a scene from a Western movie, you would be correct. Salvatore Cudia founded Cudia City as a motion picture lot in 1938 on this site, filming many Westerns and television shows before being subdivided for homes in 1950s and 1960s. **Opposite:** This excellent example of the Traditional Ranch House spreads across its lot in the offhanded manner of a house designed for informal living. Different wings are clad in different materials as if built over time; a dovecote perches over the garage; diamond-pane windows fill window bays; the roofline dips low to accentuate the low profile.

Miller House Phoenix, Arizona, 1956

Left: An original bathroom features pink and gray fixtures.
Right: The home's wall-mounted RadiOcall intercom and radio brought the housewife in the kitchen within a push button of any room in the house. With dishwashers and garbage disposals, such modern technology brought the ease of modern life to Ranch House dwellers. **Opposite:** The kitchen's natural-wood cabinets, wrought-iron pulls and hinges, and tile counters were typical of Ranch House decor in the 1950s. With the RadiOcall intercom, it provided the comforts of new technology in the comforting guise of traditional materials—a balance typical of the Ranch's moderate Modernism.

Miller House

Top: With double entry doors on the left, the open plan placed no doors between living room, family room, and kitchen. **Bottom:** The family room featured a sizable indoor barbecue. Sliding glass doors open to the trellised patio. **Opposite:** Partially buried in the ground, the long and low lines of the roofline emphasize the horizontal landscape and architecture.

Miller House

This page: In his wide-ranging career, prominent Phoenix Modernist Ralph Haver designed several tract-house models, including the Donaldson House. The small house turns its wide gable toward the street; high walls provide privacy, while large clerestory windows let light stream inside. Desert landscaping spreads across the front. **Opposite:** As in some Case Study house designs, the carport combines the entry and a patio. The Donaldsons purchased the lot and interviewed an architect, but he could not meet their budget. Instead they began to look at different tract-home models then being built in the Phoenix area. Liking Haver's design, they hired builder Fred Woodworth of Town and Country Homes to construct that model on their site, even though it was not in a tract development.

Donaldson House   Ralph Haver, Architect; Fred Woodworth, Builder   Phoenix, Arizona, 1957

Bottom: The original blueprints show the carport at the top, the living room and kitchen in the middle, and the three bedrooms at the bottom of the drawing. **Opposite:** The back-yard of the concrete-block house includes a 1962 addition, right.

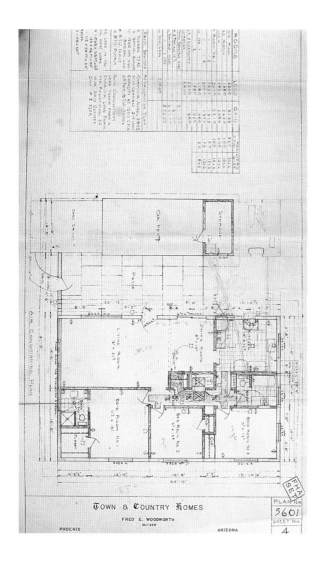

TOWN & COUNTRY HOMES

FRED E. WOODWORTH
BUILDER

PHOENIX   ARIZONA

PLAN No
5601
SHEET No
4

Left: Unlike Phoenix's citrus subdivisions, which are irrigated from the Valley of the Sun's canal system, the Donaldson House neighborhood retains the dry landscape of the native desert.
Right: The open plan includes living room and dining room. A 1962 addition, including family room and bedroom, extends off the kitchen, beyond. **Opposite:** High ceilings in the hot climate are one passive environmental design factor; the high window also frames the mountain view. The house still uses a swamp cooler, which cools by removing humidity from the air. It also allows windows and doors to remain open, unlike air conditioning, which must be used in an enclosed space.

Donaldson House

This page: In Phoenix and elsewhere outside California, this style is called the California Ranch House. It usually includes a masonry foundation rising to the window sill, traditional board-and-batten siding, shake roof, and often diamond-pane windows and a front porch. The warm materials and evocative images of this Moderate Modern architecture communicate a positive residential character to a large portion of the general public, where the factory imagery of mainstream Modern design did not. **Opposite:** The backyard was a social revolution for the millions of cramped apartment dwellers who moved to the suburbs in the 1950s. In the city, the street was often considered an unsafe and unhealthy play place for children; backyard pools, swing sets, sandboxes, and play houses allowed mothers to supervise their children and their playmates. For adults, the backyard offered other pleasures. *Sunset* magazine, often in the forefront of trends, had extolled the delights of barbecues since the 1930s. Once reserved for the ultra-rich, swimming pools became a common fixture in middle-class back-yards. Suburbanites with an appreciation of nature also formed a core of supporters for the nascent environmental movement, solidified in 1962 with the publication of Rachel Carson's *Silent Spring.* **Following spread:** The emergence of the Ranch House in the West in the late 1920s paralleled a similar rediscovery of American Colonial in the East. The Thompson House's furnishings echo that Colonial revival. Sideboards, flower-print wallpaper, Windsor chairs, wing chairs, and matched candlesticks on the mantle demonstrate that the Ranch could adapt to Traditional as easily as to Modern. Left, view from dining room to the hallway to bedrooms. Right, living room.

Thompson House   Medallion Homes, Builder   Phoenix, Arizona, 1958

Top: The kitchen has been updated with new appliances. The window looks out on the front lawn. **Bottom:** The sunroom looks out on the backyard swimming pool. **Opposite:** An original bathroom features pastel tiles and large inset sinks typical of the 1950s. **Following spread:** The Thompson House is built in a citrus subdivision, a one-time orchard sold for housing development. The substantial irrigation system that flooded the groves remains in use, providing water for residential landscaping. The lawn is graded to retain about six inches of water.

Thompson House

This page: The three-bedroom two-bath Gross House is a tract model by Allied Builders that is repeated in several Phoenix subdivisions. The architectural qualities of custom Ranch houses by noted architects like Wurster, Harris, and Ford are fairly clear. Less noted are the architectural qualities of tract homes like this one, though the success of the Ranch is largely due to such mass-produced designs. Instead of refined individual craftsmanship, tract-house design rests on its efficiency in applying modern construction materials, technology, and methods; instead of customized plans, a tract model is judged on its responsiveness to modern suburban family lifestyles. These designs are successful when they reflect the cultural forces that consistently shape residential architecture. **Opposite:** In this Contemporary Ranch design, the traditional porch posts are translated into tapered spears.

Gross House Allied Builders Phoenix, Arizona, 1957

Left: The family room at the rear of the house looks out on the sun porch and backyard. **Right:** Living and dining room look out on the front porch. **Opposite:** Added sun porch extends the interior as well as the usable outdoor space in the heat of Arizona summers.

Gross House

This page: Built for Dr. and Mrs. J. M. Woodall, Jr., the Sandra Rhodes House (like other Harris designs) turns windowless walls to the street, but opens to canyon views on the opposite side. The tree stands in a walled court off the master bedroom, the garage is to the right. The entry is at center. **Opposite:** Inside the entry gate is this open-air atrium surrounded by a pool of water, a potent symbol of relief in the hot Texas landscape.

Woodall ★ Rhodes House   Harwell Hamilton Harris, Architect   Big Spring, Texas, 1958

This page: The Woodalls hired Harris after visiting the 1954 *House Beautiful* Pace Setter House he designed for the Dallas State Fair grounds. It was also built around an atrium with an enclosed gallery. The wide eaves of the Big Spring house sheltered the windows and brick walls from the harsh sun. **Opposite, left:** This view shows the central corridor, with living room on the left and entry atrium on the right, with bedrooms at the end of the hall. Note how the hipped ceiling extends over the living room and the corridor; the screen wall allows the spaces to be joined or separated. This screen wall was also a design feature of the Pace Setter House. **Opposite, right:** The living room fireplace creates a solid, asymmetrical mass.

Woodall · Rhodes House

Left: The living room ceiling is stained Philippine mahogany. Doors open to a wide terrace jutting out over the sloping site. **Right:** Harris often used thin wood trim on ceilings to create geometric patterns, much as Frank Lloyd Wright did at the Coonley House, a masterpiece of Prairie Style architecture. **Opposite, top:** Each bedroom opens onto a deck or onto a private walled court. Note the wood trim on the hipped ceiling, echoing the living room's ceiling treatment. **Opposite, bottom:** Dining room also enjoys a private walled courtyard. Lowered soffit at the window continues outside.

Woodall · Rhodes House

This page: Most critics overlooked or ignored the prototypical Ranch House architecture, the variety of its manifestations, the social complexity of its neighborhoods, and the tract Ranch's often innovative mass-construction methods. To most critics living in traditional cities with little contact with the conditions, desires, and apparent satisfactions of middle-class suburban life, the suburbs were a foreign land. As early as 1921, influential architecture critic Lewis Mumford titled an essay "The Wilderness of Suburbia," and a century-long drum beat of anti-suburban opinion followed. John Keats derided the "fresh-air slums" fixed on "corroding everything they touch" in *The Crack in the Picture Window* in 1957. Activist/folk singer Malvina Reynolds summed up Ranch ramblers as "Little boxes made of ticky-tacky." **Opposite:** A minority view was offered by J. B. Jackson in *Landscape* magazine, and Herbert Gans in *The Levittowners*, but the negative assumptions squelched most serious assessments of this enormous suburban phenomenon, and sidelined the endeavors of architects such as Palmer and Krisel, Robert Severin, Ernest Kump, Harry C. Hall, Arthur Lawrence Millier, and others designing creatively for the real world of the building industry. The Ranch was pummeled, and yet it thrived.

Lee House   Phoenix, Arizona, ca. 1958

Top: The open plan was a major innovation that spread through the housing industry in the 1950s. The combined kitchen and dining area on the left connects with the living area on the right, as seen below. **Bottom and opposite:** The hearth remained a key focus of the Ranch House plan, as it had been to the Prairie Style house fifty years before. **Following spread:** Boston is a brownstone city and San Francisco a Victorian city. Sunbelt metropolises like Phoenix, San Jose, and Santa Ana, California, are Ranch House cities. Before World War II they had consisted of small downtowns surrounded by agricultural land; after the war, those farms became prime candidates for housing subdivisions. With the Ranch as the primary housing type of that booming era, huge areas of these cities were covered with Ranch House tracts, which remain to this day.

Lee House

Left: Now the home of Robert Lewis, this wood house was designed by Harwell Harris for Dr. and Mrs. Milton Talbot near the brick Woodall • Rhodes House on page 186. **Right:** Also inspired by the 1954 Pace Setter House Harris designed with his University of Texas students, this house welcomes visitors through a plain wall into an open-air atrium garden. **Opposite:** Here Harris used a modified board-and-batten siding that marked out the regular module he often used in designing. Widely spaced vertical boards mark the structural grid, while horizontal boards fill in between.

Talbot • Lewis House   Harwell Hamilton Harris, Architect   Big Spring, Texas, 1958

This page: One side of the house extends out over the sloping site with a wood deck. **Opposite:** The wide glass-walled gallery on the entry court links inside and outside. As at the Pace Setter and Woodall • Rhodes houses, sliding screens (right) create flexible spaces.

Talbot • Lewis House

Left: Dining room opens onto the wide wood deck. Wood trim defines the geometry of the hipped ceiling. **Right:** The regular modular structure, the reverence for wood, the subtle proportions, and even the ornamental rhythm of the lamps show Harris' appreciation of Japanese architecture, as adapted for this house in the heart of America. **Opposite:** The landscaping's smooth river stones and bamboo also refer to Japanese design.

Talbot • Lewis House

This page: The Spanish hacienda was one of the first sources of the Ranch's image and plan; later versions like this reintroduced some of the hacienda's textures of rough adobe walls and arcades.
Opposite: Desert plants mix with cultivated landscaping in this garden. The Ranch's straightforward structure with shallow roof gable lined with exposed rafter ends reflect its own mid twentieth-century vernacular.

Christiansen House Phoenix, Arizona, 1959

Top: Arcades encourage easy outdoor living. **Bottom:** Gabled living room ceiling with aluminum sliding doors are complemented by an overscaled mantle. **Opposite:** Porch creates a transition zone for outdoor living.

Christiansen House

This page: A classic Contemporary Ranch simplifies the basic Ranch forms: stone pillars redefine the traditional covered porch, while the gable end is enclosed in glass instead of wood siding.

Opposite: Foundation planters create a transition between building and landscape.

Morris House Lucian Hood, Jr., Architect Houston, Texas, 1959

Top: Stone pillar supporting gable end continues inside, as can be seen through the clerestory windows. **Bottom:** Floor-to-ceiling living room windows look out on front entry walk. **Opposite:** The *corredor*, or covered walkway circling the interior court, is left open to the air in this house, where Cliff May usually enclosed it as interior circulation space.

Morris House

This page: Also in the Cudia City Estates subdivision (like the Miller house on p. 162), the Rogers House is a custom design by the builder. Dry-desert planting, with palms, African sumac, Chilean mesquite, saguaro, and palo verde trees, complements the Ranch House in its native Western setting. **Opposite:** Front door is between the living room, left, and the master bedroom, right.

Rogers House Phoenix, Arizona, 1960

Left: Front door is shaded by a low sweeping roof, which visually links the house to the ground. **Right:** Family room at back of house features brick fireplace wall, Arcadia sliding doors. The family room was an invention, quickly spread by developers in the 1950s, as American family life became more informal. **Opposite:** Low horizontal lines of this Ranch tie it visually to the ground plane.

This page: Back in the 1930s, Cliff May helped to define the Ranch as a picturesque, carefully edited version of the historic hacienda. By the late 1950s, however, the simplifying influence of Modernism influenced May to abstract his Ranch designs and exaggerate the scale of his roofs—though still creating a romantic picture. The Wayne and Peggy Bemis House, built for Dr. Harold Eshelman, is an example of May's design in this period. The living room, with its own patio and glimpses of the Pacific Ocean, is on the left, behind the extended stucco wall.

Opposite: The great roof sweeps close to the ground. Its post-and-beam structure creates a large trellis over the swimming pool. The center of the house is open, creating an unobstructed view through to the living room and its patio.

Eshelman ⋆ Bemis House Cliff May, Designer   Rolling Hills, California, 1963

Left: The welcoming front door is as carefully composed as ever in May's designs. Widely spaced battens march across the board siding, and a pot bench for brightly colored geraniums leads the way to the deeply carved Spanish doors. **Right:** The rear courtyard is surrounded by tall sheets of glass that visually vanish, tying together inside and outside. Radiant heat in the floor continues outside. The dining room's baroque Spanish chandelier is original. The ceilings are deeply raked plaster. **Opposite:** Living room focuses on the large fireplace, framed by thick molding. The slump block adobe walls are lightly plastered, letting the rough texture of the blocks to show through—a romantically crude visual theme through the house.

Eshelman • Bemis House

Top: Two views of the rear covered court: at top, the slight enclosure of the glass walls emphasizes the openness of the house. Baroque iron bar stools are original furnishings.
Bottom: From the living room, the space extends to the pool and garden and beyond to a panoramic view of Los Angeles. As in May's Evans House, a skylight runs down the ridge line. The simplified forms are exaggerated, but given scale with ornate corbels at the top of the posts. **Opposite:** At night the site at the ridge top of the Palos Verdes peninsula looks north to downtown Los Angeles.

Eshelman • Bemis House

Left: Bedrooms have tall sloping ceilings, but are brought down to human scale by the soffits with indirect lighting. Master bedroom has its own garden patio, a signature May feature. **Right:** Kitchen counter pass-through looks out to pool court. **Opposite, left:** Typically picturesque May elements include roughly carved wood window grills. **Opposite, right:** As do most houses in Rolling Hills, the Eshelman • Bemis House has a stable.

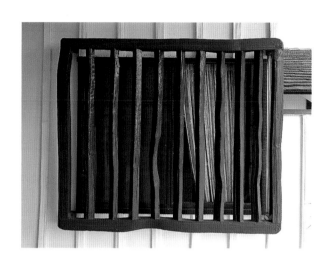

Left: The Ranch House was a constant favorite in the mass-circulation shelter magazines of America. This house by O'Neil Ford was designated *House and Garden* magazine's House of Ideas #14. The evolution and variety of the Ranch House—from custom homes to tracts, from Traditional to Contemporary, from Harris to Wurster to May to Palmer and Krisel to Mogenson, from Lakewood to Rolling Hills, from Burns to Webb to Sharp—belies the oft-repeated critique of the Ranch as a bland and false architecture. It is time for the Ranch to take its place as one of the most successful residential types and a major part of the story of twentieth-century architecture. **Right:** With its covered porches, this two-story house modernizes the two-story houses David Williams and O'Neil Ford designed thirty-five years earlier, based on vernacular working-ranch houses. **Opposite:** Though heavily forested, the house blends with its site.

Burdine House   O'Neil Ford, Architect   Houston, Texas, 1968

Left: Simple wood paneling with minimal trim and carved fireplace surround repeat elements for which Ford is known. **Right:** Dining room.

Opposite: Plank walls and tall bedsteads take rustic vernacular elements and artfully exaggerate them.

Burdine House

As late as 1978, the *Custom Home Plans Guide* included a "truly Western Approach to the Ranch House," an 1,830-square-foot house with Ranch elements such as a "long loggia," "post and braces," "handsplit shake roof," and "two wings sprawl[ing] at an angle on either side of a Texas-sized Hexagonal living room." Plan P-1113 revealed Mexican influences in its heavily textured stucco walls, but assured readers that "the interior arrangement is completely tuned to the requirements of contemporary living."[1]

By this time, however, the Ranch House was already on its way out as America's most popular home. Changing tastes coupled with more expensive land costs cut back on the luxuriant sprawl of the Ranch House. Master-planned communities like Irvine, California, introduced a new version of suburbia. More blows came from the constant attacks by academics on suburbia in general and the Ranch House in particular as symbols of American anomie, isolation, and cultural barrenness. As the 1980s arrived, new owners demolished their modest, low profile Ranch houses in favor of larger houses with dramatic two-story entries and Mediterranean styles; the Ranchburger was replaced by the McMansion.

At present, an impressive formality has returned—at least on the exterior. Once again, formal dining rooms are a fixture in upscale homes and grand circular staircases suitable for debutante balls are common. Yet, the Ranch House's informal family room, with flowing spaces adjoining the outdoor patio or terrace (much reduced in size because of increased land prices), remains an indispensable part of the American home—enhanced today by the technology of the entertainment center such as wide-screen televisions and DVDs.

In the history of twentieth-century architecture, the Ranch House must be recognized as one of the most successful and widespread residential types. The open plan suited modern lifestyles perfectly; the cowboy myth resonated in the rustic materials and the wide-open spaces of the backyard; and mass-production methods (plus progressive financing by the FHA and the lending industry) kept prices within range of the vast majority of the population. Whether it was Harwell Harris's *House and Garden* Pace Setter House in Dallas or a Kaiser Ranch in Panorama City, the democratized Ranch House had something to offer to each class of American.

As architecture, the Ranch House squarely addressed some of the most ambiguous and compelling aspects of twentieth-century culture. The question was this: how to achieve a balance between the human desire for individual expression *versus* the enormous, complex, and interdependent nature of a mass economy and culture.

Pushed through the sieve of Taylorism, Fordism, and then Kaiserism, the symbol of rural isolation became the very fabric of communal suburbia. We desired a home of our own, on a property we could control, but we lived ten feet from our neighbors. We desired privacy and a style that expressed our unique individuality; but we lived in a society where mass consumerism offered the defining choices, based on its ability to deliver luxuries at affordable prices—as long as enough people would buy them. We wanted to live amid nature, but we were in congested cities.

The Ranch House artfully straddled all these contradictions. It offered the image and message of the self-reliant cowboy life, which came prepackaged in movies, songs, myths, and finally our houses. And it offered these iconic images, convincingly, in mass quantities, thanks to the application of modern construction organization, machines, and materials. Essentially, the self-sufficient Ranch was transmuted in its application to sophisticated mass-production methods and its great replication in the landscape. The Ranch House mastered the use of symbols, carefully attenuating them without draining their meaning. How minimal does the suggestion of a dovecote, porch, and board-and-batten wall need to be in order to still convey the idea that this is indeed a Ranch? The answer is in the public consciousness. Architecture is a cultural expression, a fact that the Ranch House fully embraced.

Modernism has long pointed to technology as the key factor that changed life in the twentieth century. But Modernist architecture often stumbled by assuming that people wanted to live in buildings that celebrated, reflected, and even worshiped the machine—architecture that saw itself in the machine's likeness. The popularity of the Ranch

House is one of several trends in the twentieth century that suggests a different conclusion. Like the movies (that essential twentieth-century technology), the Ranch House focused not on the machinery that produced the wonder, but on its product: the Platonic shadows laden with meaning flickering on the cave wall. Just as few people sit in a movie theater to watch the projector, few people choose a home to admire the nailing pattern.

And so the inventions of the twentieth century—the suburban homestead rendered accessible by car, the mass-produced, single-family middle-market home, the casual lifestyle permitted by sliding glass doors and kitchen appliances, the instantly recognizable images of the Roy Rogers show—permitted the Ranch House to exist.

The remarkable impact and significance of the Ranch House should raise questions about the real nature of twentieth-century architecture. While it is often assumed that high-art theory and design trickle down—compromised and coarsened in the process—to be made available to the general public, in fact the opposite occurs at least as frequently. The Ranch House is an example. The solid, practical vernacular working-ranch houses of the nineteenth century served as inspiration to Wurster, May, Ford, Williams, and others; the efficient methods of David Bohannon, Fritz Burns, John F. Long, and other merchant builders brought prefabrication and modern plans to the masses, not because they were echoing the high-art Modern Case Study or Eichler homes, but because they had arrived at these techniques through their own efforts to build sensibly and meet the tastes of the public. Apparently, things trickle up, too.

There was indeed cross-pollenization between high-art and popular design, but the process was more complex than the trickle down theory presumes. Bill Krisel admired Walter Gropius and Konrad Wachsmann's General Panel System, but as their development of the system went nowhere in the building industry, Krisel and partner Dan Palmer (both trained as Modernists) had the imagination and desire to make a modular system work in the very practical world of mass-produced housing. Their work—filled with creative accommodations and adjustment to the commercial building and marketing process—fulfilled Modernism's goal of bringing decent design to the general public. They made it work, and thus they have a place in the story of twentieth-century architecture.

At present, Ranch House neighborhoods are fast changing. Like the Victorian row houses that were bulldozed willy-nilly in the 1950s, the Ranch House value does not endure. And yet a quick survey reveals that Ranch neighborhoods have generally stood the test of time. Rollingwood, David Bohannon's wartime housing in Richmond, California, is still a blue collar community and maintains its original quality. The houses have stood well over sixty years, without dilapidation or decay. Individual touches have been added—new siding, occasional expansions—but, overall, they are less changed than the middle-class Ranch subdivisions. Lakewood Rancho Estates, the May-Choate tract in Long Beach, California, likewise remains a stable community, with a large percentage of original owners still living in the neighborhood. Here too, additions have changed many houses over the years; while some are unrecognizable, some owners are, today, restoring these well-designed homes to their original character.

Phoenix's Maryvale development by John F. Long remains a solid lower-middle-class community. It is still an important entry point for homebuyers seeking an affordable first home—just as it was in 1954. Though hardly gentrified, it plays a vital and healthy role in the city. It indicates why the Ranch House tracts of fifty years ago are best welcomed into the urban mix, and not bulldozed for another conceit.

Theories of urban design change. The 1950s suburb was a solution to the congested, crime-ridden, parkless inner city. Today, New Urbanism considers the Ranch suburbs (with houses that turn their back to the street) problematic. However, Rollingwood, Panorama City, Westchester, and San Lorenzo Village suggest that we do not need to shun our suburban past; rather, we need to understand it and build on the very real strengths—architectural, urbanist, and social—that it already possesses.[2]

The question we must address is: How do we rejuvenate Ranch neighborhoods today?

Notes

Introduction

1. Royal Barry Wills. *Better Houses for Budgeteers: Sketches and Plans by Royal Barry Wills*. New York: Architectural Book Publishing Co., Inc., 1941, p. 6.

2. Brendan Gill. "Reflections: The Horizontal City," *The New Yorker* (September 15, 1980): 143.

3. John P. Dean and Simon Breines. *The Books of Houses*. New York: Crown Publishers, 1946, p. 52.

4. Cliff May, *House Beautiful*, April 1946.

5. "Who Wouldn't Like to Live Here?" *Good Housekeeping*, January 1953, p. 94.

6. Royal Barry Wills. *Living on the Level: One-Story Houses by America's Best Liked Architects*. Boston: Houghton Mifflin Company, 1955, p. 105.

7. "All American Rambler for Pleasant Living," designed by Harold J. Bissner, Pasadena, in William J. Hennessey, *America's Best Small Houses*. New York: The Viking Press, 1949, p. 185.

8. *National Homes of Moderate Cost*. USA: National Plan Service, Inc., 1949, p. 3, 5.

9. Author's interview with John F. Long, October 13, 2003.

10. For more discussion of the Ranch House as the major housing type creating a city, see Grady Gammage, Jr., *Phoenix in Perspective: Reflections on Developing the Desert*. Tempe: Herberger Center for Design Excellence, 1999, p. 39.

11. Merry Ovnick. *Los Angeles: The End of the Rainbow*. Los Angeles: Balcony Press. 1994. p. 254.

12. See Greg Hise, Robert Bruegmann, Richard Longstreth, D. J. Waldie, Merry Ovnick, Grady Gammage, Hal Rothman, etc.

13. Dean and Breines, p. 68.

14. Lisa Germany. *Harwell Hamilton Harris*. Berkeley: University of California Press, 2000, p. 105.

15. T. H. Robsjohn-Gibbings. *Homes of the Brave*. New York: Alfred A. Knopf, 1954, p. 81.

16. Paul Adamson and Marty Arbunich. *Eichler: Modernism Rebuilds the American Dream*. Salt Lake City: Gibbs Smith, Publisher, 2000, p. 27.

Chapter 1

1. The historic examples that follow are taken from Alan Hess and Alan Weintraub, *Rancho Deluxe* (San Francisco: Chronicle Books, 1999), pp. 20; 46; 62. The Harrell Ranch house was moved to the Ranch Museum at Texas State University in Lubbock, Texas.

2. Esther McCoy and Evelyn Hitchcock, "The Ranch House," in *Home Sweet Home: American Domestic Vernacular Architecture*, eds. Charles Moore, Kathryn Smith, Peter Becker (New York: Rizzoli, 1982), p. 84. The country haciendas, according to Esther McCoy, were based on the form of town homes built in pueblos from San Diego to Sonoma: one- and two-story buildings, usually U-shaped. "Ranch houses were handsomely sited in a gently rolling landscape, the long low lines bespeaking the generous use of ground in the sprawling floor plan, the wings stretching out but enclosing, the private and public spaces harmoniously defined, The houses continued to turn an almost blank side to the public view, while creating intimate spaces in courts"; Esther McCoy and Evelyn Hitchcock, "The Ranch House," in *Home Sweet Home*, p. 88.

3. The movement for a new home architecture was spurred by nineteenth-century social reformers, who often focused on improved housing as a solution to urban crime, disease, and poverty. The 1876 Philadelphia Fair displayed model worker housing; the Philadelphia row house had been a great attraction at the 1893 Columbian Exposition in Chicago, where the single-family home, planned efficiently and accessible to the middle class, was well received. As important as the development of the architecture was the supply of financing, which made it possible for the middle class to purchase a home.

4. Other Wright examples of these ideas include the Isabel Roberts house, the Robie House, and the Barton House in Buffalo.

5. Esther McCoy with Randell L. Makinson, *Five California Architects* (New York: Praeger Publishers, 1960), p. 109.

6. The Bandini House would be admired by William Wurster, a key contributor to the Ranch style in the 1930s; see Robert Winter, "William Wilson Wurster," by Tim Andersen, p. 251. Other Craftsman-era houses that explored the U-shaped, one-story plan inspired by the Mission style are Henry Greene's 1913 Crowe House in Pasadena and Frederick Louis Roehrig's 1905 house for Chicago lawyer Arthur Jerome Eddy in Pasadena, which used plain stucco-covered walls emulating adobe, as Cliff May would thirty years later in his Ranch House designs; see Robert Winter, "Frederick Louis Roehrig" in *Toward a Simpler Way of Life: The Arts and Crafts Architects of California*, Robert Winter, ed (Berkeley; University of California Press, 1997), p. 114.

7. The Curtis Ranch in the foothills above Pasadena would be admired by modernist Harwell Hamilton Harris twenty years later; see Lisa Germany, *Harwell Hamilton Harris*, p. 47.

8. Tim Andersen. "Louis B. Easton," in *Toward a Simpler Way of Life*, pp. 155-156. Other wood post-and-beam Craftsman designs that relate to forms later seen in the Ranch House include architect Francis T. Underhill's 1903-1904 house for himself in Montecito, which simplified the multiple roofs usually found in the Craftsman bungalow into a single broad-eave roof lined with exposed rafters; architect Emmor Brooke Weaver's 1910 Easton bungalow, 1911 Cook bungalow, and 1911 Barron ranch in the San Diego area (Alexander D. Bevil, "Emmor Brooke Weaver," in *Toward a Simpler Way of Life*, pp. 211-213); architect Henry Gutterson's 1915 house for Sophie McDuffie in Berkeley, with a plan that opens the living room directly onto the garden; "Viewed from the garden," observes historian Susan Dinkelspiel Cerny, "the scale and massing of the house, the shape of its roof, the placement of its windows, and its proximity to the ground all combine to anticipate the broad, one-story ranch-style homes that became popular after World War II." (Susan Dinkelspiel Cerny, "Henry Gutterson" in *Toward a Simpler Way of Life*, p. 76.)

9. This growing culture of popular taste and consumerism was already well established in palatial department stores and the popular press.

10. Robert Winter, *The California Bungalow* (Los Angeles: Hennessey and Ingalls, 1980), p. 32.

11. In Chicago, the bungalow took on a distinct form that proved long lasting in popularity. Derived from nineteenth-century workers' cottages, with an ornamental relationship to the Prairie Style, most were brick on narrow city lots that were twenty-five to thirty-three feet wide. The plan typically placed the living room, dining room, and kitchen on one side of the lot, and two or three bedrooms on the other side. With full indoor plumbing and central heating, "they were, in many ways, the first really 'modern' houses for the working class," writes historian Robert Bruegmann; see HYPERLINK http://tigger.uic.edu/depts/ahaa/imagebase/buildings/. Built from the 1910s on, the Chicago bungalows are found in the Bungalow Belt—a concentric circle four to eight miles from the central Loop, reflecting the next step in housing development as that prairie city expanded.

12. Edward R. Bosley, "Sylvanus B. Marston," in *Toward a Simpler Way of Life*, pp. 174-175.

13. Charles Sumner Greene, "Impressions of Some Bungalows and Gardens," *The Architect* 10 (December 1915): 252, 278.

14. McCoy and Hitchcock, p. 88.

15. Lauren Weiss Bricker, "Roland E. Coate: Furthering an Architectural Inheritance," in *Johnson Kaufmann Coate: Partners in the California Style* (Santa Barbara: Capra Press, 1992), p. 49.

16. The editorial staff of *Sunset Magazine* in collaboration with Cliff May. *Sunset Western Ranch Houses* (Menlo Park: Lane Publishing Company, 1946), p. 18.

Chapter 2

1. The cult of the West had been born, even as pioneers were still moving west and Native Americans and buffalo populated the plains. Zane Grey and Ned Buntline novels before the turn of the century paved the way for traveling Wild West shows—vaudeville shows with a cowboy and Indian theme, starring Pawnee Bill, the 101 Ranch, and Buffalo Bill Cody himself. Dude ranches were emerging as favored vacation spots, often on authentic working ranches that needed the extra income; see Alan Hess and Alan Weintraub, *Rancho Deluxe* (San Francisco: Chronicle Books, 2000), pp. 11-12.

2. Los Angeles was adept at melding historical imagery with radically modern spaces; the city was perfectly at ease with the transformation of adobe haciendas into gas stations, car washes, and drive-in markets; see Longstreth, *The Drive-in, the Supermarket, and the Service Station*, p. xvii.

3. As always in architectural history, it is difficult to identify a single "first" Ranch House. The Gregory Farmhouse's fame is at least as dependent on its promotion in the media (then and since)—articles in *Sunset* and a *House Beautiful* award in 1931—as on its architectural ideas. Though it does combine vernacular images and structures with a modern attitude toward plan and aesthetics, it was built only three years after Roland Coate's Tweedy House, and a year before Clarence Tantau's 1928 Armsby Ranch House in Carmel Valley, both of which had strong similarities as collections of simple geometric forms in rustic materials.

4. Wurster admired the U-plan of the Bandini House by the Greene brothers; see Robert Winter, *Toward a Simple Life*, Tim Andersen, p. 251.

5. *An Everyday Modernism: The Houses of William Wurster. Berkeley*, ed. Marc Treib (Berkeley: University of California Press, 1995), p. 19.

6. Howard Barnstone, *The Architecture of John F. Staub, Houston and the South* (Austin: University of Texas Press, 1979), pp. 38-39.

7. Daniel Gregory, "William W. Wurster," in *Toward a Simpler Way of Life*, p. 250.

8. Daniel Gregory, "William W. Wurster," in *Toward a Simpler Way of Life*, p. 253.

9. The Gallway House is included in Cliff May's 1946 defining book on Ranch Houses, p. 105, Photo 73. Other examples of Wurster Ranch Houses in the 1930s are the 1932 Donald Gregory House in Scotts Valley, the 1935 Nayler Residence in Oakland, and the 1940 Chickering House in Woodside.

10. Author's interview with Richard Peters, February 18, 2003; Marc Treib, ed., *An Everyday Modernism*, p. 169.

11. Mary Carolyn Hollers George, *O'Neil Ford, Architect* (College Station: Texas A&M University Press, 1992), p. 19.

12. David R. Williams, "An Indigenous Architecture: Some Texas Colonial Houses." *Southwest Review* 14 (October 1928): 67.

13. Doug Tomlinson and David Dillon, *Dallas Architecture 1936-1986* (Austin: Texas Monthly Press, 1985), p. 58, 61.

14. German settlers in New Braunfels and Fredericksburg arrived under the organization of Prince Carl of Solms-Braunfels, founder of the German Immigrant Society in the 1850s. The visionary prince had planned the colony to the smallest details, including the design of safe, secure housing.

15. Muriel Quest McCarthy, *David R. Williams: Pioneer Architect* (Dallas: Southern Methodist University Press, 1984,) p. 43. O'Neil Ford was slightly less romantic than Williams about the aesthetic intentions of the early immigrants. "I began to discern that this was a different type of architecture. It wasn't German because there were Germans here. It wasn't Polish because there were a lot of Poles; not Mexican because there were a lot of Mexicans or Spanish. The missions . . . that's all there was that was really sharing with the Spanish. The rest of it was a highly interesting indigenous architecture and looked the way it did because of the lack of materials. Whatever materials they had were all they had to use and they weren't trying to copy things in the old country." Mary Carolyn Hollers George, *O'Neil Ford*, p. 19.

16. George, *O'Neil Ford*, p. 23.

17. Hanson, born in 1893 in the agricultural town of Ontario in the foothills of the San Gabriel Mountains, was a landscape architect who helped to guide the hallmark plantings of Palos Verdes, as well as gardens for Edward Doheny, Harold Lloyd, and Mary Pickford in Beverly Hills. With an eye for picturesque plants, he had been drawn—as had many others—to the gorgeous scene created by Bernard Maybeck at the Palace of Fine Arts at the 1915 Pan Pacific Exposition in San Francisco.

18. A. E. Hanson, *Rolling Hills: The Early Years February 1930-December 7, 1941* (Rolling Hills: City of Rolling Hills, 1978).

19. "New residences and additions to existing residences shall conform as closely as possible to the concept of the traditional or contemporary California ranch-style house located in Rolling Hills," defined as "single floor dwellings, low in profile . . . rambling in character" with "low pitched roofs with shake-like appearance with wide overhangs." *Building Zone Regulations,* Rolling Hills Community Association of Rancho Palos Verdes, December 18, 1997.

20. David Bricker, "Ranch Houses Are Not All the Same," in Deborah Slaton and William G. Foulks, eds., *Preserving the Recent Past 2* (Washington, D.C.: Historic Preservation Education Foundation, 2000), pp. 2-119.

21. Williams (1890-1962) was born in a half-dugout covered in poles, straw, and sod in the Texas Panhandle, where he started photographing sod houses as early as 1907. He trained as a mechanical engineer before entering the University of Texas at Austin, leaving in 1916 just short of a degree. After working as an engineer in Mexico, he took time off to study art and architecture in Europe, attending the New York School of Fine and Applied Arts in Paris.

22. "A Rambling Texas Home," *American Home* (January 1935): p. 70; Wayne Gard. "The Ranch-House Goes to Town," *Better Homes and Gardens* (June 1937): p. 32.

23. Muriel Quest McCarthy, *David R. Williams: Pioneer Architect* (Dallas: Southern Methodist University Press, 1984), p. 49.

24. George, *O'Neil Ford*, p. 22.

25. McCarthy, *David R. Williams*, p. 46. Williams's first houses reflected the Spanish tradition popular in Texas, and abstracted versions of Georgian. But his F. N. Drane House (1928-29) in Corsicana was stone and brick, wide, and low, with a pronounced tile roof.

26. Designing relief communities first for the Texas Civil Works Organization, Williams then worked for the New Deal when President Roosevelt's aid Harry Hopkins invited him in 1934 to work in Washington on the problem of rural rehabilitation. Williams's work, now national in scope, still often drew on regional architectures as well as Modern ideas. He and Ford also helped restore La Villita in 1940, a small historic district of San Antonio considered a decrepit slum. During World War II he helped develop defense housing, working with Louis Kahn, Oskar Stonorov, and George Howe in Philadelphia, Eliel and Eero Saarinen in Detroit, and Richard Neutra in San Diego. Most of these were two-story apartment block units. McCarthy, *David R. Williams*, pp. 121, 137.

27. McCarthy, *David R. Williams*, p. 49.

28. David Bricker, "Cliff May," in *Toward a Simpler Way of Life*, p. 285. David Bricker's excellent work on Cliff May, including his dissertation at the University of California, Santa Barbara, is essential research on this important California designer.

29. David Bricker, "Cliff May," in *Toward a Simpler Way of Life*, p. 285.

30. The editorial staff of *Sunset* magazine in collaboration with Cliff May, *Sunset Western Ranch Houses* (Menlo Park: Lane Publishing Company, 1946), p. 31.

31. Though May's homes in the 1930s were furnished in Mission-style or moderate contemporary designs, in the 1950s and 1960s he often used heavily carved Spanish-style credenzas, with baroquely worked carved doors and wrought iron chandeliers. *Sunset* publisher Mel Lane bought furniture from William Randolph Hearst's estate at San Simeon for his office in a Cliff May-designed building. See also the Santa Barbara design by architect Glenn H. Marchbanks Jr. for Mr. and Mrs. Ray Kroc, *Architectural Digest* (Fall 1968): 18-31; interior design by Jamie Ballard.

32. Daniel Gregory, "Living with Lariats: Cliff May and Sunset Magazine," paper for symposium on Cliff May's eightieth birthday, March 5, 1988, note 3.

33. By 1931, Ford had seen Wurster designs in architecture magazines. At the same time Ford was also discovering the work of Alvar Aalto, and came increasingly under the influence of Modernism; in 1939, he met Richard Neutra and William Wurster in California, and hosted Neutra on a tour of Texas the next year.

34. Lisa Germany, *Harwell Hamilton Harris*, p. xi.

35. Germany, *Harwell Hamilton Harris*, p. 108.

36. Even closer to the common ranch house was Lloyd Wright's 1936 Raymond Griffith Ranch House in Woodland Hills, in the San Fernando Valley.

37. The editorial staff of *Sunset* magazine in collaboration with Cliff May, *Sunset Western Ranch Houses*, p. ix.

38. A review of plan books, and professional and museum publications shows not only that Ranch style was well established by 1940 in custom home design in the southwest, but that it was being increasingly built by architects across the rest of the country in a variety of sizes and variations. Examples from Editors of Architectural Forum, *The 1940 Book of Small Houses* (New York: Simon and Schuster, 1939) include the 1939 Ranch House for Mrs. Moye W. Stephens by Theodore Criley, Jr., in La Verne, California (pp. 25-27); a 1939 Florida house by architect Robert Smith (p. 41); architect Chalfant Head's own 1939 house in Ojai (p. 78); architect Robert H. Ainsworth's R. R. Bush House in Palm Springs (p. 67); architect Gilmore and Ekman's Modern house for Dr. W. P. Sherrill in Phoenix (p. 68); Marston and Maybury's Cape Cod-style Arnold R. White House in Pasadena (p. 92); and the Traditional Ranch House by Allen

G. Siple's for Mrs. L. B. Fleishman in Los Angeles (p. 96.) This book also includes a number of unbuilt designs that show the direction of future Ranch House designs, influenced by the Prairie Style and Modern forms and details.

39. Among other architects who designed Ranch houses were John Byers, Palmer Sabin, Roland Coate, H. Roy Kelley, and Sumner Spaulding in Southern California; Robert Stanton, Carl Gromme, Michael Goodman, Mario Corbett, John Yeon in Northern California; Van Evera Bailey, William Bain, and Pietro Belluschi in the Pacific Northwest.

40. David Gebhard and Robert Winter, *The Guide to Architecture in San Francisco and Northern California* (Salt Lake City: Gibbs Smith Publisher, 1985), p. 579.

41. The Editors of *The Architectural Forum, The 1940 Book of Small Houses*, pp. 20-21.

42. See James Ford and Katherine Morrow Ford, *The Modern House in America* (New York: Architectural Book Publishing, 1940), pp. 113-114.

43. Born in Knoxville, Tennessee in 1892, Staub studied architecture at MIT, returning to Houston in 1921. Like California architects such as John Byers, Lutah Maria Riggs, and Palmer Sabin (Staub's roommate at MIT) the majority of his buildings were traditional in styles such as Georgian, Colonial, Louisiana Plantation, Greek Revival, French Regency, and, later, Modern; Ranch was one more style in his repertoire. *Architecture* magazine identified a one-story Spanish-style adobe home by California architect Palmer Sabin as "A California Ranch House" in January 1935.

44. An example is Elm Grove, the Hollamon House in Seguin, Texas, dating from the 1850s; see Dorothy Kendall Bracken and Maurine Whorton Redway, *Early Texas Homes* (Dallas: Southern Methodist University Press, 1956) p. 30.

45. Barnstone, *The Architecture of John F. Staub*, p. 210.

46. "The ranch house had been introduced in Houston during the late thirties, but not until the postwar years, a period of tremendous physical expansion, did it emerge as the dominant type of detached housing unit," writes historian Howard Barnstone (Barnstone, *The Architecture of John F. Staub*, p. 49). Other Texan examples include architect Bartlett Cocke's 1939 San Antonio house for George Bailey Peyton (Editors of Architectural Forum, *The 1940 Book of Small Houses*, p. 28) and architect Arthur Thomas's "basic one-floor house" in Dallas, Texas in 1946 (John P. Dean and Simon Breines, *The Books of Houses* (New York: Crown Publishers, 1946), p. 93).

47. Greg Hise, *Magnetic Los Angeles: Planning the Twentieth-Century Metropolis* (Baltimore: The Johns Hopkins University Press, 1997), p. 141.

48. Marlow-Burns and Company, Realtors, Owners, and Developers was formed in 1938. Fred W. Marlow studied engineering at West Point and MIT and served in World War I before moving to Los Angeles and entering a career in real estate. He was appointed the first FHA district director for Southern California and Arizona during the Depression, strengthening his contacts with officials in government and finance. Fritz Burns (1899-1979), was already involved with real estate while in high school in Minneapolis, attended the University of Minnesota and the Wharton School of Finance at the University of Pennsylvania before arriving in Los Angeles in 1921. Successfully speculating in the real-estate boom of that decade, he was first set back by the Depression's downturn, but later prospered by selling the depleted oil deposit under his land holdings. In the 1960s, he continued to develop housing with Kaiser and independently, co-owned Kaiser's Hawaiian Village resort in Waikiki, and was vice-chairman of the Hilton Hotel Corporation. He also owned a reindeer ranch in the San Fernando Valley, which supplied white European fallow deer to Southern California shopping centers at Christmastime. (Greg Hise, *Magnetic Los Angeles*, p. 243.; also a 1945 biography by W. C. Rodd, publicity director of Kaiser Community Homes, Henry J. Kaiser Archives; Honolulu *Star Bulletin*, June 1, 1965.)

49. Greg Hise, *Magnetic Los Angeles*, p. 138.

50. Greg Hise, *Magnetic Los Angeles*, p. 136. Hise explains the step-by-step evolution of Marlow-Burns (echoed by developers elsewhere) that turned real estate lot sellers into housing developers. In effect, they were preparing themselves for the tremendous boom to come after World War II.

51. The Depression did little to encourage the risk of building houses in large numbers, but did spur the Federal government's efforts to help the home building industry with easier financing and formulating basic housing standards. Since the Hoover administration, the government's policy encouraged homeownership as the firm foundation for a stable society, and industry followed suit. The 1934 Federal Housing Administration (FHA) guaranteed housing loans, encouraging private developers to risk larger developments. The FHA also developed design guidelines for a small but efficient house, which would meet their approval—a tremendously influential design for developers dependent on easy loans. Some of these ideas were applied directly to federally-funded projects.

52. Greg Hise, *Magnetic Los Angeles*, p. 69.

53. Greg Hise, *Magnetic Los Angeles*, p. 67.

54. Greg Hise, *Magnetic Los Angeles*, p. 136.

55. Author's interview with Frances Bohannon Nelson, June 9, 2003.

56. Marc Treib, ed. *An Everyday Modernism*, p. 145; Hise. *Magnetic Los Angeles*, p. 7.

57. Placing housing tracts near jobs was a key part of progressive planning. As Greg Hise has shown, the larger, trend-setting housing developers built near the aerospace and automotive factories that drove the postwar economy. It is not random chance that placed the May-Choate subdivisions in Cupertino near Sunnyvale's Lockheed, in Long Beach near Douglas Aircraft, and in Pomona near General Dynamics. The middle-management engineers were the target audience for such homes, which had a sophisticated plan and were priced above the tracts of Lakewood and Kaiser Community housing nearby.

58. Hise, *Magnetic Los Angeles*, p. 138.

59. *San Francisco Examiner*, June 7, 1941.

60. Bohannon was a patron of sculptor Beniamino Bufano, who created many of his rounded granite sculptures for Hillsdale Shopping Center in 1956.

61. *Architectural Forum* (June 1945).

62. Bohannon built a model house at 9333 Murillo Avenue and advertised it in the newspapers to attract customers. With his office on Market Street in San Francisco, he also reached over to Marin County in 1937, opening a branch office in Kentfield as the Real Estate Services Company.

63. Gardner Dailey (1895-1967) was a respected Bay Area architect and Berkeley and Stanford student who, with Wurster and others, explored the line between vernacular wood contractor construction and the clean structural expression of Modernism. Besides custom homes, Dailey also designed a home fitting strict FHA standards, published in *Life* magazine in 1940; Bohannon built some at his Belle Haven development. One of his Bay Area houses was included by Cliff May in his first book on Ranch style. Dailey's work illuminates a point of intersection between high-art Modernism and the Ranch House style.

64. "The Story Behind the Good Housekeeping Home in Woodside Hills," brochure, 1939. Good Housekeeping Studio of Architecture, Building and Furnishings, Helen Koues, director.

65. *San Mateo Times and Dailey News Leader*, March 29, 1940.

66. John P. Dean and Simon Breines, *The Book of Houses*, p. 85. Hugh Stubbins Jr. designed defense housing at Windsor Locks, Connecticut. The simple gabled one-story duplexes might be taken as Ranches, but are more likely to be interpreted as Cape Cods by Eastern buyers: unpainted vertical board siding covered the eaveless boxes, with a simplicity that was affirmatively Modern.

67. Hise, *Magnetic Los Angeles*, p. 142. Title VI of the Housing Act, passed March 1941, gave home builders incentives to build for the small-house market in areas where defense industries were predicted to cause housing shortages.

68. The Levitts built 2000 units of low-cost defense housing in Norfolk, Virginia during the war.

69. "The Story of San Lorenzo Village: a David D. Bohannon Organization Development," *American Builder* reprint, Bohannon archives, 1943.

70. *Practical Builder*, Chicago, December 1943.

71. San Lorenzo Village was planned by Ronald Campbell, a San Mateo planning engineer and consultant working for Bohannon on wartime projects; he remained with the Bohannon organization after the war. The design team included civil engineer Edwin Smith, and planner Lucien Stark. (*Architectural Forum*. June 1945.)

72. Also notable: San Lorenzo Village included the first Mervyn's Department Store, and a church designed by architect Bruce Goff, moved from its original location at Camp Parks army base in San Ramon where he was stationed during World War II. Using the vernacular Quonset hut of army construction, Goff created a handsome Modern design that suited the modern town of San Lorenzo Village.

73. See Roger Montgomery in *Bay Area Houses*, pp. 229-264; Greg Hise in *An Everyday Modernism*, pp. 138-163.

74. *Blueprints for Modern Living: History and Legacy of the Case Study Houses* (Museum of Contemporary Art, Los Angeles, 1990), p. 94.

75. See Marc Treib, editor. *An Everyday Modernism*, pp. 145-153.

Chapter 3

1. Robert C. Elliott, *San Francisco News*, August 1, 1945.

2. Merry Ovnick, *Los Angeles: The End of the Rainbow* (Los Angeles: Balcony Press, 1994), p. 289.

3. Tom Riley, *Popular Mechanics Build-it-yourself Ranch-type House* (Chicago: Popular Mechanics Press, 1951), p. ii. Whalen also designed embassies in Washington, D.C., and the home of columnist Drew Pearson in Virginia, as well as West Coast Ranch houses.

4. *Collier's* (January 11, 1947): 40.

5. The history of these postwar developers in shaping American cities represents a large gap in our general understanding of twentieth-century architecture. A few of note include: Frank Sharp in Houston; Albert Balch, Seattle; Lawrence Weinberg of Larwin, San Francisco Bay Area; T&S Construction, in Phoenix, Denver, Salt Lake City, and Los Angeles; Walter R. Sant & Sons for The McCarthy Company, Los Angeles; Del Webb, Gibralter Construction, Hallcraft, John T. Hall, Ralph T. Staggs, and Womack in Phoenix; Samuel Hoffman in Phoenix and Chicago; Earl Smith in Richmond, California; Brown and Kaufman in San Francisco; Mackay Homes, San Francisco.

6. Among other high-art architects' solutions for mass-producable housing were Buckminster Fuller's Dymaxion House, and Bauhaus colleagues Walter Gropius and Konrad Wachsmann's elaborate General Panel System for prefabricated homes. It continues to appear in many architectural histories, though its impact on the housing industry was virtually nonexistent. "This single story design exudes logic and dullness," wrote David Gebhard and Robert Winter, and they are right; the system created boxy and uninspired spaces. [David Gebhard and Robert Winter, *Los Angeles: An Architectural Guide* (Salt Lake City: Gibbs Smith Publisher, 1994), p. 164.] William Wurster (with architect Ernest Kump) also explored the prefab home in the Prebilt House, which used synthetic resins for tapered laminated plywood arches that could be quickly erected on a slab. The same system could be used for houses or schools. It created a neat rectangular house with a gentle gable. It also went nowhere; see Treib, ed., p. 155. Wurster's Case Study #3 incorporated elements that accommodated mass reproduction more than the other Case Study houses, but it also went nowhere as a working model.

7. Gropius's office, The Architects Collaborative, did build a cooperative tract of Modern homes in Five Fields, Lexington, Massachusetts in 1953; see Katherine Morrow Ford and Thomas Creighton, *Quality Budget Houses: A Treasury of 100 Architect-designed Houses from $5,000 to $20,000* (New York: Reinhold Publishing Corporation, 1954) p. 159.

8. Ironically, the traditional role of architects in creating American housing was also reduced by the mass produced homes.

9. New York City native Joseph Eichler (1900-1974) moved to the Bay Area in 1925, where he worked for Nye and Nisson, Inc., a wholesaler of butter and eggs, until he left the business in 1942 during World War II. After living in a Frank Lloyd Wright Usonian house in Hillsborough during part of World War II, he became enthused with building houses. He ran the Sunnyvale Building Company beginning in 1947, first using plan services but then hiring an architect. Meeting and hiring University of Pennsylvania graduate architects Stephen Allen and Robert Anshen, he built more Modern designs; their first in 1949 was 1,044 square feet, with three bedrooms, selling for $9,500. By 1952, Eichler was selling five hundred homes a year, and by 1954, 1,800 buildings a year. After 1951, A. Quincy Jones and Frederick Emmons joined Eichler, and later Claude Oakland also worked with Eichler. These architects provided Eichler with a variety of models over the years; many, with flat roofs, large expanses of glass walls, and Modern formal compositions are comfortably Modern in style; they avoided board-and-batten and other typically Ranch elements. But the simple Eichler homes with single gable roofs, exposed post-and-beam structure, and open plans are remarkably close in spirit to the tract homes of May and Choate, and Palmer and Krisel. All these designs shared vernacular and modern California precedents.

10. See *Blueprints for Modern Living*.

11. The floor plan of the first Case Study house built, by J. R. Davidson in 1946, placed two bedrooms on one side and the combined living room-dining area on the other, eliminating the traditional halls in a manner "much copied by developers in the 1950s," observed Esther McCoy, but in fact this arrangement was a feature of the FHA plan seen in defense housing and early tract developments [*Blueprints for Modern Living: History and Legacy of the Case Study Houses* (Museum of Contemporary Art, Los Angeles), p. 37.]

12. Between 1941 and 1945, Kaiser's Richmond shipyards produced an astonishing 747 ships. Kevin Starr, *Embattled Dreams: California in War and Peace 1940-1950* (New York: Oxford University Press, 2002), p. 147.

13. Raymond K. Graff, Rudolph A. Matern, and Henry Lionel William, *The Prefabricated house: A Practical Guide for the Prospective Buyer* (Garden City, New York: Doubleday and Co., 1947), p. 1.

14. Greg Hise, *Magnetic Los Angeles*, p. 168.

15. Kaiser dishwashers and disposals were found in both Case Study houses and Panorama City houses, a spectrum indicating the real spread of Modernism. Appliances were interchangeable pieces, bringing technology to daily life—to be regularly updated as they improved. See *Blueprints for Modern Living*, p. 174; Greg Hise, *Magnetic L.A.* pp. 169-170.

16. Greg Hise. *Magnetic Los Angeles*, p. 169.

17. House assembly lines had been considered even before the war; Dallas Ranch House architect Charles Dilbeck worked on such a scheme in 1939 when he collaborated with industrial designer Norman Bel Geddes on prefabricated housing of steel frame and stucco walls, which sold for $35 a month with a car included. Funded by the Ford Foundation, the project stopped when the war began. [Doug Tomlinson and David Dillon, *Dallas Architecture 1936-1986* (Austin: Texas Monthly Press, 1985, p. 50.] In the mid 1930s the federal government supported the development of prefabricated houses for the Tennessee Valley Authority. (Raymond K. Graff, Rudolph A. Matern, and Henry Lionel William. *The Prefabricated house: A Practical Guide for the Prospective Buyer*. Garden City, New York: Doubleday and Co., Inc. 1947, p. 1.) The all-steel Lustron homes ($9,000 not including land and installation) made a heroic effort, but did not dent the housing market. [Gwendolyn Wright, *Building the Dream: A Social History of Housing in America* (Cambridge: MIT Press, 1981), p. 245.]

18. William J. Hennessey, *America's Best Small Houses* (New York: The Viking Press, 1949, p. 7).

19. Burns built the house himself, but Kaiser also used it in their publicity. Greg Hise, *Magnetic Los Angeles*, p. 256. The house still stands, presently converted to offices, at the corner of Wilshire Boulevard and Highland Avenue.

20. Greg Hise, *Magnetic Los Angeles*, p. 196.

21. Greg Hise, *Magnetic Los Angeles*, pp. 205-206.

22. The humble Chicago bungalow evolved, with a face lift, into the Raised Ranch after 1945: still on a narrow urban lot, usually with the same division of bedroom and living areas, it adopted the cleaner, wider eaves and hipped roofs of the Ranch, rendered in yellow, red, or tan brick. Its full basement lifted the main floor off the ground, giving it its name. Though it bore little resemblance to the luxurious spreads that Cliff May was designing around the world, the Ranch label stuck.

23. Polish-born Mark Taper moved to England and made money building houses in the 1930s; he moved to Los Angeles in 1939. He bought American Savings and Loan Association in 1950, and owned Biltmore Homes. Louis Boyar had built houses in nearby Long Beach during the 1930s. Ben Weingart was owner of Aetna Construction Co. The Montana Land Company first laid out a subdivision on the site in 1929. Houses were built as ranchettes, with land for chicken coops. A golf course and clubhouse opened in 1933, and a two-year college nearby in 1935. But by 1937 only twenty-seven houses had been built; see D. J. Waldie, *Holy Land*, p. 62, 74.

24. All was not socially progressive, however. While Fritz Burns sought a diverse mix of occupations in his developments to support the idea of a community, he maintained racial restrictions. (Greg Hise. *Magnetic Los Angeles*, p. 205.) Rollingwood, the housing tract built by David Bohannon in 1942 for Kaiser shipyard workers, experienced threats when the first Negro moved into the neighborhood in 1952: Wilbur D. Gary, a Navy war veteran, refused to move with his seven children; the sheriff had to disperse the crowd in an incident reported in newspapers around the Bay Area. (*San Francisco Chronicle*, March 5, 1952.)

25. Like Panorama City, Lakewood was planned as a community—not just a bedroom tract—from the start. Weingart built Lakewood Shopping Center, hiring A. C. Martin to design the handsome new May Co. department store, with the M high above its parapet. It opened in February 1952. On 264 acres, it claimed to be the largest shopping center in the world. Beside the anchor store, one-story buildings with stores clustered around the base and along outdoor pedestrian walkways.

26. Cliff May, *House Beautiful*, April 1946.

27. The editorial staff of *Sunset* magazine in collaboration with Cliff May, *Sunset Western Ranch Houses* (Menlo Park: Lane Publishing Company, 1946), p. 11.

28. See Walter Curt Behrendt's design for Norwich, Vermont, in Thomas H. Creighton, *Homes Selected by the Editors of Progressive Architecture* (New York: Reinhold Publishing Corporation, 1947), p. 42; William J. Hennessey, *America's Best Small Houses* (New York: The Viking Press, 1949), p. 185.

29. Examples of custom Ranch houses across the country in Thomas H. Creighton, *Homes Selected by the Editors of Progressive Architecture* (New York: Reinhold Publishing Corporation, 1947): a Lake Oswego Ranch by Van Evera Bailey, who worked with Modernists from William Gray Purcell to Richard Neutra (p. 24); William Hempel's design for Atherton, California (p. 68); Charles W. Lorenz's in Glendale, Missouri (p. 71); Sheldon Brumbaugh's Klamath Falls design (p. 78); Antonin Raymond's design in Westport, Connecticut, for J. Delano Hitch (p. 115); William C. Suite and Roscoe L. Wood's design for Eugene D. Vinogradoff in Artures, Virginia (p. 170). Also worthy of further study is Arthur T. Brown in Tucson and Lucian Hood Jr. in Texas.

30. Hennessey, *America's Best Small Houses*, p. 11.

31. David Gebhard, "Harwell H. Harris," in *Toward a Simpler Way of Life*, p. 281.

32. Joseph Barry, *The House Beautiful Treasury of Contemporary American Homes* (New York: Hawthorn Books, Inc., Publishers, 1958), p. 52.

33. Other Ford houses influenced by the Ranch aesthetic include the 1952 Berger and Tinkle houses in Dallas, the 1953 US Gypsum Research Village House in Barrington, Illinois, and the 1956 Dallas house for Patrick Haggerty, a large Ranch-style house with broad standing-seam metal roofs that hugged the landscape. Ford also designed a daring 1956 factory with hyperbolic paraboloid roofs for Texas Instruments, which Haggerty founded.

34. The ongoing influence of the Prairie Style and Usonian houses can also be seen in Buford Pickens's design for the A. W. Rosenau House in Detroit, Michigan, reflecting the Prairie Style with wide eaves under a hipped roof and horizontal unpainted wood siding; also in Robert F. Bishop's house in Wallingford, Pennsylvania. [Thomas H. Creighton, *Homes Selected by the Editors of Progressive Architecture* (New York: Reinhold Publishing Corporation, 1947), p. 180, 182.]

35. The Editors of *Progressive Architecture*, *Homes*, p. 93.

36. See also the Neils House, Minneapolis, 1949; the Anthony House, Benton Harbor, Michigan, 1949; the Keys House, Rochester, Minnesota, 1950; the Schaberg House, Okemos, Michigan, 1950; the Mathews House, Atherton, California, 1950; the Smith House, Hefferson, Wisconsin, 1950, the Kinney House, Lancaster, Wisconsin, 1951, and the Lamberson and Alsop houses in Oskaloosa, Iowa, 1951.

37. The sliding door required new technology to make it practical. Though it had been a staple of Modernism—Richard Neutra's 1935 Beard House in Altadena, for one, featured a massive steel-framed window wall that pulled back to unite living room to garden—it remained an expensive and impractical solution for mass-produced tract homes until the invention of the light weight aluminum door.

38. The editorial staff of *Sunset* magazine in collaboration with Cliff May, *Sunset Western Ranch Houses* (Menlo Park: Lane Publishing Company, 1946,) p. 111.

39. Starr, *Embattled*, p. 143.

40. *San Jose Mercury News*, February 8, 1949, p. 1.

41. His competition in Northern California included Henry Doelger (developer of San Francisco's Richmond District), the Stoneson Brothers, and Standard Homes, who all used the same system. Williams and Burrows built 600 homes of the modified Ranch type in Mills Park off Kains Ave.; Conway and Culligan built San Mateo Village.

42. In 1946, Bohannon bought tracts of redwood timber near Eureka in Northern California so that he would be assured of wood; as president of Dolly Varden Lumber Company in Arcata, he also owned his own lumber mills. Though he discovered that the purchase was not cost effective (he sold it in 1955), it served a purpose when a ready supply of lumber kept construction flowing smoothly through the fluctuations in suppliers' industries; Bohannon would swap his timber for nails or bath tubs—anything to stay in business. (*San Mateo Times*, January 23, 1946; *Colliers*, January 11, 1947, p. 40.)

43. The large purchasing power of a large developer was a major factor in lowering costs. "We were in a position to negotiate," said Phoenix developer John F. Long. "I was always price-wise way below the market," still allowing a profit of $500 per house. Even with the huge demand for housing immediately after the war, developers struggled. "Some, like Kaiser Community Homes of Los Angeles, are plugging along but have found it difficult to attain the goals they set for themselves. In 1946-1947, Kaiser-Burns built 5,000 of 6,000 planned; in 1948 they built 299 of 3,000 planned. Bohannon had built 900 homes in 1947," reported the *Wall Street Journal* (February 8, 1949): 1.

44. *Blueprints for Modern Living*, p. 37. In Phoenix, developer John F. Long found that the soil of the west valley where Russian immigrant farmers had settled, was better for building than the east side. Through family connections with those landowners, he was able to obtain a large amount of land at a good price as a necessary foundation for his company.

45. *San Francisco News*, May 27, 1950; *San Francisco Chronicle*, June 4, 1950.

46. Keeping up the publicity heat, *Better Homes and Gardens*'s "Idea Home" for 1955 was by Mogens Mogenson AIA of Burlingame. It was the $26,950 home of David E. Bohannon, David D. Bohannon's son. A modern post-and-beam design of respectable skill, it was another trial balloon to attract attention, while Bohannon's tracts continued to be respectably and popularly Ranch style. (*San Mateo Times*, November 5, 1955; *San Francisco Chronicle*, September 9, 1956.)

47. Unidentified newspaper clipping, Bohannon archives.

48. Mogenson, born in Copenhagen and educated in Denmark, maintained his own private practice while working for Bohannon.(*San Francisco Daily Pacific Builder*, October 12, 1956.)

49. Choate was a talented architect according to his competitor Dan Palmer. A graduate of the USC School of Architecture, he later taught at UCLA. He also designed sets for movies and television.

50. Over 18,000 of the May-Choate homes were built. Stern and Price were the developers of the first 300 homes in Cupertino in 1952, selling for $7,500-$10,000. Other developers built in Vista, Bakersfield, and Chico in 1953, Tucson in 1954, Denver and Anaheim in 1955, Pomona in 1957; the 1954 Long Beach development near Lakewood was developed by Ross Cortese, developer of the Leisure World retirement communities.(*Sunset* Magazine, November 1952; *House + Home*, October 1952, March 1955, November 1958.)

51. *House + Home* (March 1955): 51.

52. Palmer and Krisel also sued one client for using their plans without permission. They won on the basis that the architect owned their intellectual property—the design reflected in the drawings. The drawings embodying the design were copyrighted; after consideration, Palmer and Krisel decided that they could not patent the system itself.

53. *House + Home* (March 1953): 134.

54. *AIA Journal* (September 1961): 27.

55. *AIA Journal* (September 1961): 27.

56. In later years, Fickett designed resort hotels, spas, apartments, and the Los Angeles Harbor cargo and passenger terminals. See obituary, *Los Angeles Times* (June 19, 1999): A22.

57. *House + Home* (March 1953): 133.

58. His clients in this period included Spiros Ponty in West Los Angeles, Johnson, Tyson & Lynds in Whittier, and Mac-Bright in La Habra.

59. *House + Home* (March 1953): 132.

60. Plan services like L. C. Majors designed models for $10-$25 per house. In comparison, Fickett designed twenty models for Sherman Park, from which the developer picked six. For this work Fickett received a flat retainer of $3,500 plus a royalty of $35 per house built—a total of $16,450 for the tract's first 370 houses. The contract stated that the plans could not be used elsewhere unless with consent. These fees varied; for another developer of 160 houses, Fickett received $75 per house. On another he charged $30 per house, plus the $2,600 retainer, for 120 houses. [*House + Home* (March 1953): 138, 172 , 173.] Anshen and Allen received $100 per house as royalty on Eichler houses. (Adamson, *Eichler*, p. 66.) Palmer and Krisel received $1000; their fee per house plotted (not just constructed) was adjusted if they also did the plot plans. Palmer and Krisel reported half a million in fees by 1955. (Author's interview with Dan Palmer, July 31, 2002.) "The architect should not expect to clear a profit on the preparation of drawings, but derive all his profit from royalties obtained each time the house is repeated," said Fickett. [*House + Home* (March 1953): 173.]

61. *House + Home* (March 1953): 137.

62. *Los Angeles Times Home Magazine*, March 10, 1957

63. Palmer knew Entenza before he came to California; earlier Entenza had published a house Palmer designed in *Arts + Architecture*.

64. Dan Palmer and William Krisel distinguish between their Modern designs and Ranch houses: in their definition a Ranch House is a wood-stud structure built by conventional building methods, as at Lakewood. As defined in this book, their tract designs ranged from Contemporary Ranch to Modern; often the distinguishing characteristic was the roofline: gabled ridges implied "Ranch," while butterfly or flat roofs, overtly modern forms, implied "Modern."

65. The 274-home tract (which included one Krisel had purchased) had four plans varying from 1,200 square feet to 1,400 square feet, and four different elevations for each plan. At 1400 square feet, they sold for $14,900 including the lot in 1954, or seven dollars per square foot for construction.

66. Author's interview with Dan Palmer, April 25, 2003. "As students we were thrilled," says Krisel, with USC professor Konrad Wachsmann's General Panel System, developed with Walter Gropius in the late 1940s. (Author's interview with William Krisel, July 22, 2003.) The systems of Gropius and other high-art architects did not interest bankers and developers, and Gropius and the others did not make a serious attempt to understand their concerns. But Krisel, with Palmer, adapted what they had learned with their own keen appreciation for the commercial housing industry.

67. The young architects formed a partnership; they associated with Welton Becket Associates on Mt. Sinai hospital; John Lindsay joined the firm as partner for one year.

68. In his subdivision projects, Krisel wanted to introduce a greenbelt, but he was not able to achieve it until the Sandpiper in Palm Desert years later; they did, however, eliminate the alley that the city usually insisted on. The house was then oriented to the garden in the back, with the carport or garage in the front.

69. Beginning in 1956, Palmer and Krisel began to build in Palm Springs for Robert and George Alexander. The Twin Palms tract was the first in a series of striking Modern tracts, featuring glass walls, butterfly roofs, carports, and clerestory windows in the desert city. Across the nation, Palmer and Krisel worked with forty different builders. Other clients included Liberty Homes in Pomona, Harlan Lee, Bollenbacher and Kelton, Sanford Adler, Jim Smith and Travis Kleefeld, Larwin, Marlborough Homes, and Dunas Greene and Dunas in Reseda. The office in Los Angeles had sixty employees in the 1950s, with ten more in the San Diego office they opened in 1958.

70. This and subsequent quotes are from author's interview with John F. Long, October 13, 2003.

71. Paul Adamson and Marty Arbunich, *Eichler: Modernism Rebuilds the American Dream*. (Salt Lake City: Gibbs Smith, Publisher, 2000), p. 108.

72. In 1950 Long built 300 houses; by 1953 two thousand were built when his largest development, Maryvale, opened; and, by 1959, 2,500; between 1947 and 1975 he built 30,000 houses in the Phoenix region. (Gammage, p. 46.)

73. Talbot Hamlin. "'What Makes it American' Architecture in Southwest and West," *Pencil Points* 20 (December 1939): 773-775.

74. Marc Treib, ed. *An Everyday Modernism*, p. 74.

75. Russell Hitchcock, "An Eastern Critic Looks at Western Architecture," *California Arts and Architecture* (Dec. 1940): 20, 41.

76. Elizabeth B. Mock, *If You Want To Build A House* (New York: Simon and Schuster, Inc., 1946); George Nelson and Henry Wright, *Tomorrow's House* (New York: Simon and Schuster, 1945).

77. Lisa Germany, *Harwell Hamilton Harris* (Berkeley: University of California Press, 1991), p. 123.

78. Esther McCoy, *The Second Generation* (Salt Lake City: Gibbs M. Smith, Inc., 1984), p. 81.

79. Other relevant Ford designs include the 1962 Cecil Green residence in Dallas, and the 1968 Lawrence House (with Ford associate Chris Carson) in Patagonia near Tucson, Arizona.

80. Tomlinson and Dillon, pp. 48-52.

Epilogue

1. *Custom Home Plans Guide* 123 (Winter 1978); Mineola, New York: Master Plan Service, Inc. plan P-1113.

2. Grady Gammage Jr., *Phoenix in Perspective: Reflections on Developing the Desert*. (Tempe: Herberger Center for Design Excellence, 1999), p. 147.

Selected Bibliography

"A Rambling Texas Home," *American Home* (January 1935), p. 70.

"An Experience in Modern Living–Ranch Style," *Architectural Digest* (Fall 1968) pp. 18-31.

"Better Homes and Gardens presents Six Idea Homes of the Year," *Better Homes and Gardens* (September 1958), pp. 45-59.

"Big Dave Bohannon, Operative Builder by the California Method," *Fortune* 33, no. 4 (April 1946), pp. 144-147, 190-200.

"Bohannon Building Team," *Architectural Forum* 82, no. 6 (June 1945), pp. 133-136, 138, 142, 146.

"The Story of San Lorenzo Village: A David D. Bohannon Organization Deyelopment," *American Builder* (1943).

"Who Wouldn't Like to Live Here?" *Good Housekeeping* (January 1953), pp. 93-97.

Adamson, Paul and Marty Arbunich. *Eichler: Modernism Rebuilds the American Dream.* Salt Lake City: Gibbs Smith, Publisher, 2002.

Barnstone, Howard. *The Architecture of John F. Staub, Houston and the South.* Austin, Texas: University of Texas Press, 1979.

Barry, Joseph. *The House Beautiful Treasury of Contemporary American Homes.* New York: Hawthorn Books, Inc., Publishers, 1958.

Blueprints for Modern Living: History and Legacy of the Case Study Houses. Cambridge, Massachusetts: The MIT Press, 1989.

Bracken, Dorothy Kendall and Maurine Whorton Redway, *Early Texas Homes.* Dallas: Southern Methodist University Press, 1956.

Bricker, Lauren Weiss, "Roland E. Coate: Furthering an Architectural Inheritance," in *Johnson, Kaufmann, Coate: Partners in the California Style.* Santa Barbara: Capra Press, 1992.

Bricker, David, "Ranch Houses Are Not All the Same," in *Preserving the Recent Past 2,* Deborah Slaton and William G. Foulks, eds. Washington, D.C.: Historic Preservation Education Foundation, 2000.

Buckner, Cory. *A. Quincy Jones.* London: Phaidon, 2002.

Callender, John Hancock. *Before You Buy a House.* New York: Crown Publishers, Inc., 1953.

Creighton, Thomas H., Frank G. Lopez, Charles Magruder, and George A. Sanderson. *Homes Selected by the Editors of Progressive Architecture.* New York: Reinhold Publishing Corporation, 1947.

Custom Home Plans Guide #124, Mineola, New York: Master Plan Service Inc. (Winter 1978).

Dean, John P. and Simon Breines. *The Book of Houses.* New York: Crown Publishers, 1946.

Dillon, David. *The Architecture of O'Neil Ford: Celebrating Place.* Austin: University of Texas Press, 1999.

Editorial staff of *Sunset Magazine* in collaboration with Cliff May. *Sunset Western Ranch Houses.* San Francisco: Lane Publishing Co., 1946.

Editorial Staff of *Sunset* Magazine and Books. *Western Ranch Houses by Cliff May.* San Francisco: Lane Publishing Co., 1958.

Editors of *Architectural Record. A Treasury of Contemporary Houses.* New York: F. W. Dodge Corp., 1954.

Editors of *Architectural Forum. The Book of Low Cost Houses.* New York: Simon and Schuster, Inc., 1940.

———. *The Book of Small Houses.* New York: Simon and Schuster, 1936.

———. *The 1940 Book of Small Houses.* New York: Simon and Schuster, Inc., 1939.

Eichler, Ned. *The Merchant Builders.* Cambridge: MIT Press, 1982.

Ford, James and Katherine Morrow Ford. *The Modern House in America.* New York: Architectural Book Publishing Co., Inc., 1940.

Ford, Katherine Morrow and Thomas Creighton. *Quality Budget Houses: A Treasury of 100 Architect-designed Houses from $5,000 to $20,000.* New York: Reinhold Publishing Corporation, 1954.

Fox, Stephen. *Houston Architectural Guide.* Houston: The American Institute of Architects/Houston Chapter, 1990.

Gammage, Grady Jr. *Phoenix in Perspective: Reflections on Developing the Desert.* Tempe: The Herberger Center for Design Excellence, College of Architecture and Environmental Design, 1999.

Gard, Wayne, "The Ranch-House Goes to Town," *Better Homes and Gardens* (June 1937), p. 32.

Garden City Co. of California. *Ideal Homes in Garden Communities.* New York: Robert M. McBride and Co., 1916.

Garlinghouse Ranch and Suburban Homes, Topeka, Kansas: L. F. Garlinghouse Co., Inc., eighth edition, c. 1958.

Gebhard, David. *Schindler.* New York: The Viking Press, 1971.

———, "The Suburban House and the Automobile," in *The Car and the City: The Automobile, the Built Environment, and Daily Urban Life,* Martin Wachs and Margaret Crawford, eds. Ann Arbor: The University of Michigan Press, 1992.

Gebhard, David and Robert Winter. *Architecture in Los Angeles: A Complete Guide.* Salt Lake City: Gibbs M. Smith, Inc., 1985.

———. *A Guide to Architecture in Los Angeles & Southern California.* Salt Lake City: Peregrine Smith, Inc., 1977.

———. *The Guide to Architecture in San Francisco and Northern California Architecture.* Salt Lake City: Gibbs M. Smith, Inc., 1985.

Gebhard, David and Harriette Von Breton. *L.A. In the Thirties.* Salt Lake City: Peregrine Smith, Inc., 1975.

George, Mary Carolyn Hollers. *O'Neil Ford, Architect.* College Station: Texas A&M University Press, 1992.

Germany, Lisa. *Harwell Hamilton Harris.* Berkeley: University of California Press, 2000.

Graff, Raymond K., Rudolph A. Matern, and Henry Lionel William. *The Prefabricated House: A Practical Guide for the Prospective Buyer.* Garden City, New York: Doubleday and Co., 1947.

Greene, Charles Sumner, "Impressions of Some Bungalows and Gardens," *The Architect* 10 (December 1915), pp. 252, 278.

Gregory, Daniel, "Living with Lariats: Cliff May and Sunset Magazine," paper for symposium on Cliff May's eightieth birthday (March 5, 1988).

———, "Visions and Subdivisions: *Sunset Magazine* and the California Ranch House." *Architecture California* 13, no. 1 (February 1991), pp. 32-35.

Gropp, Louis Oliver, ed. *House and Garden Plans: 124 Best-Selling House Designs.* New York: The Conde Nast Publications, 1978.

Group, Harold E., ed. *House-of-the-Month Book of Small Houses.* Garden City, New York: Garden City Publishing Co., Inc., 1946.

Hamlin, Talbot, "'What Makes it American:' Architecture in Southwest and West," *Pencil Points* 20 (December 1939), pp. 773-775.

Hanson, A.E. *Rolling Hills: The Early Years, February 1930 through December 7, 1941.* Rolling Hills: City of Rolling Hills, 1978.

Hennessey, William J. *America's Best Small Houses.* New York: The Viking Press, 1949.

Hess, Alan and Alan Weintraub. *Rancho Deluxe: Rustic Dreams and Real Western Living.* San Francisco: Chronicle Books, 2000.

Hess, Alan and Andrew Danish. *Palm Springs Weekend.* San Francisco: Chronicle Books, 2001.

Hise, Greg. *Magnetic Los Angeles: Planning the Twentieth-Century Metropolis*. Baltimore: The Johns Hopkins University Press, 1997.

Home Owners' Catalogs. New York: F. W. Dodge, 1950.

Jackson, J. B. *Landscapes: Selected Writings of J. B. Jackson*. Amherst: The University of Massachusetts Press, 1970.

Jones, A. Quincy Jr. and Frederick E. Emmons. *Builders' Homes for Better Living*. New York: Reinhold Publishing Co., 1957.

Keane, James Thomas. *Fritz Burns and the Development of Los Angeles: The Biography of a Community Developer and Philanthropist*. Los Angeles: Loyola Marymount University and Historical Society of Southern California, 2001.

Koues, Helen, "The Story Behind the Good Housekeeping Home in Woodside Hills," brochure, *Good Housekeeping Studio of Architecture, Building and Furnishings*, (1939).

_____. *How to Choose, Plan and Build Your Own Houses*. New York: Tudor Publishing Co., 1946.

Lieurance, I. G. *America's Best Low Cost Homes*. Topeka, Kansas: L. F. Garlinghouse Co., c. 1940.

Longstreth, Richard. *The Drive-In, the Supermarket, and the Transformation of Commercial Space in Los Angeles, 1914-1941*. Cambridge: MIT Press, 1999.

Master House Plan Book. St. Cloud, Minnesota: Small House Planning Bureau, 1972.

McCarthy, Muriel Quest. *David R. Williams: Pioneer Architect*. Dallas: Southern Methodist University Press, 1984.

McCoy, Esther and Evelyn Hitchcock. "The Ranch House," in *Home Sweet Home: American Domestic Vernacular Architecture*, Charles W. Moore, Kathryn Smith, and Peter Becker, eds. New York: Rizzoli International Publications, Inc. 1983.

McCoy, Esther. *Five California Architects*. New York: Praeger Publishers, 1960.

_____. *The Second Generation*. Salt Lake City: Gibbs M. Smith, Inc., 1984.

Mock, Elizabeth B. *If You Want To Build A House*. New York: Simon and Schuster, Inc., 1946.

Moore, Charles, Peter Becker and Regula Campbell. *The City Observed: Los Angeles*. New York: Vintage Books, 1984.

National Homes of Moderate Cost. National Plan Service, Inc., 1949.

National Economy Homes Engineered for Substantial Savings. National Plan Service, Inc., 1949.

Prize Homes. Chicago: Wilcox & Follett Co., 1946.

Nelson, George and Henry Wright, *Tomorrow's House*. New York: Simon and Schuster, 1945.

Nequette, Anne M. and R. Brooks Jeffery. *A Guide to Tucson Architecture*. Tucson: The University of Arizona Press, 2002.

New Homes Guide #60. New York: Holt, Rinehart and Winston, 1968.

Normile, John. *Better Homes & Gardens' 1942 Edition of New Ideas for Building Your Home*. Des Moines: Meredith Publishing Co., 1942.

Normile, John and John Bloodgood, "Better Homes and Gardens' Idea Home Four Ways," *Better Homes and Gardens* (September 1959).

Obst, Frances Melanie. *Art and Design in Home Living*. New York: The MacMillan Co., 1963.

Ovnick, Merry. *Los Angeles: The End of the Rainbow*. Los Angeles: Balcony Press, 1994.

Randall, Gregory C. *America's Original GI Town: Park Forest, Illinois*. Baltimore: The Johns Hopkins University Press, 2000.

Riley, Tom. *Popular Mechanics Build-it-yourself Ranch-type House*. Chicago: Popular Mechanics Press, 1951.

Roberts, Allen. *Historic Homes of Phoenix: An Architectural & Preservation Guide*. Phoenix: City of Phoenix Publication, 1992.

Robsjohn-Gibbings, T. H. *Homes of the Brave*. New York: Alfred A. Knopf, 1954.

Rothman, Hal. *Neon Metropolis: How Las Vegas Started the Twenty-First Century*. New York: Routledge, 2002.

Rowe, Peter G. *Making a Middle Landscape*. Cambridge: MIT Press, 1991.

Starr, Kevin. *Embattled Dreams: California in War and Peace 1940-1950*. New York: Oxford University Press, 2002.

The Book of 100 Homes. St. Paul, Minnesota: Brown-Blodgett Co., 1940.

The New Book of Celotex Homes. Chicago: The Celotex Corporation, 1954.

Tigerman, Stanley, "The Postwar American Dream," in *Architecture in Context*, exhibit catalog. Chicago: Graham Foundation for Advanced Studies in the Fine Arts and the Arts Institute of Chicago, 1985.

Tomlinson, Doug and David Dillon. *Dallas Architecture 1936-1986*. Austin: Texas Monthly Press, 1985.

Treib, Marc, ed. *An Everyday Modernism; The Houses of William Wurster*. Berkeley: University of California Press, 1995.

Waldie, D. J. *Holy Land: A Suburban Memoir*. New York: W. W. Norton and Co., 1996.

Weintraub, Alan. *Lloyd Wright: The Architecture of Frank Lloyd Wright, Jr*. New York: Harry N. Abrams, Inc., Publishers, 1999.

Williams, David R., "An Indigenous Architecture: Some Texas Colonial Houses." *Southwest Review* 14 (October 1928), p. 67.

Wills, Royal Barry. *Better Houses for Budgeteers: Sketches and Plans by Royal Barry Wills*. New York: Architectural Book Publishing Co., Inc., 1941.

_____. *Living on the Level: One-Story Houses by America's Best Liked Architects*. Boston: Houghton Mifflin Co., 1955.

_____. *Houses for Homemakers*. New York: Franklin Watts, Inc., 1945.

Winter, Robert. *The California Bungalow*. Los Angeles: Hennessey & Ingalls, 1980.

Winter, Robert, ed. *Toward a Simpler Way of Life: The Arts & Crafts Architects of California*. Berkeley: University of California Press, 1997.

Woodbridge, Sally, ed. *Bay Area Houses*. Salt Lake City: Gibbs Smith, Publisher, 1988.

Wray, Diane, "Arapahoe Acres: Preserving a Post-War Modernist Subdivision," in *Preserving the Recent Past 2,* Deborah Slaton and William G. Foulks, eds. Washington, D.C.: Historic Preservation Education Foundation, 2000.

Wright, Gwendolyn. *Building the Dream: A Social History of Housing in America*. Cambridge: MIT Press, 1981.

Index

Numbers in *italics* refer
to illustrations.

Index